THE STRUGGLE FOR ⌐
from
Community Relations *to* Community Cohesion

The Story of Bradford 1950-2002

For Ann Cryer
with best wishes
Ramindar Singh
15/07/03

Ramindar Singh

THE STRUGGLE FOR RACIAL JUSTICE
from
Community Relations *to* Community Cohesion

The Story of Bradford 1950-2002

Ramindar Singh

First published 2002

Ramindar Singh, 66 Chatsworth Road, Pudsey, West Yorkshire, LS 28 8JX, United Kingdom
E-mail: ramindar@kehar.freeserve.co.uk

ISBN 0 907734 61 8

Printed by Print Plus Uk Ltd.
Design House, 2 Bolling Road, Bradford,
West Yorkshire, BD4 7BA
Telephone: 01274 305555 Fax 01274 725700

LIST OF ILLUSTRATIONS

page

DEDICATION

Dedicated to all those who have worked towards achieving racial justice in Bradford with a sense of social responsibility and wisdom.
And to my wife Dalbir, daughters Harpreet and Gurjit, grandsons Neeraj and Karam, and my sons-in-law Sanjai and Parjinder.

ABBREVIATIONS

AYM	Asian Youth Movement
BCCCI	Bradford Consultative Council for Commonwealth Immigrants
BDRRP	Bradford District Race Review Panel
BMEC	Black and Minority Ethnic Communities
BREC	Bradford Racial Equality Council
CAB	Citizens' Advice Bureau
CIAC	Commonwealth Immigrants Advisory Council
CRC	Community Relations Council
CRE	Commission for Racial Equality
CRO	Community Relations Officer
DPAC	Drummond Parents' Action Committee
LA	Local Authority
LAM	Local Administrative Memorandum
LEA	Local Education Authority
NCCI	National Committee for Commonwealth Immigrants
RAT	Racism Awareness Training
REO	Race Equality Officer
RJC	Racial Justice Council
RRA	Race Relations Act
RRAG	Race Relations Advisory Group
T&A	Telegraph & Argus
VLC	Voluntary Liaison Committees
WYREC	West Yorkshire Racial Equality Council

ACKNOWLEDGEMENTS

I owe a debt of gratitude to a number of friends and colleagues who I have worked with locally and nationally in their efforts towards achieving racial justice in Britain and developing harmonious relations between diverse ethnic groups, particularly in Bradford. Without their continuous support and encouragement, it would have been difficult to document the story of the struggle for racial justice in Bradford.

I am also indebted to Robert Walters for a very supportive, careful and critical editing of the contents for the final published form. It goes without saying that any inaccuracies and omissions, and interpretation of policies and events are solely my responsibility.

I am also grateful to the Telegraph & Argus and Tim Smith for their permission to use the photographs.

Finally, I am profoundly obliged to my daughters, Harpreet and Gurjit for their unswerving encouragement and to my wife Dalbir for her unrelenting patience when I was researching and writing this book. They always allowed me, most graciously and generously, to devote all the time I needed to work with commitment in the cause of good race relations locally and nationally.

CONTENTS

XI

PREFACE

There is no particular landmark, event or a date, to signify arrival of the first group of post-War II immigrants from the New Commonwealth countries into Bradford. In popular memory the story of these immigrants begins in the early years of the 1950s. Thus the current publication could mark the half-century point of their presence in Bradford. This is a good enough reason to share with readers the story of those events and the efforts of a large number of individuals working through a wide range of organisations in making the life for the new comers to the city fair and just.

For me, there is another reason for writing this book too. I was actively involved in the Bradford Racial Equality Council (and its predecessor Community relations Councils) since its formation in 1967. When the Bradford Racial Equality Council (BREC) was formally closed in March 2000 I felt a sense of duty almost, to document briefly the history of the BREC, that has remained a pivotal point in race related activities in the city. My initial intention was a narrow one, simply to write the life story of BREC. As I started researching for the book I was convinced that it would be inappropriate to present the life history of the BREC without looking at the broad race relations situation in the city.

The BREC was not operating in the vacuum, entirely independently or on its own. The national Community Relations Commission and the Commission for Racial Equality that provided part of its funds significantly influenced its overall approach to race-relations issues. Its activities were determined and directed to a significant level by the local events and the policies of other local institutions, particularly, the Bradford Metropolitan District Council. Hence, it became essential and appropriate to include a brief account of the policies and practices of the BREC's main funding organisations, that is, the Commission for Racial Equality and the Bradford Metropolitan District Council. With the omission of this information an assessment of the BREC's contribution towards the achievement of racial justice in the city would be incomplete and unfair.

The research and the first draft of the book were completed before the Bradford Council and the Bradford Vision set up the Bradford Race Review in November 2000. However, two major events in the city, the most devastating race riots in July 2001 and the publication of the findings of the Bradford Race Review in the form of the Ouseley Report made it necessary to update the original draft to take account of these major developments. As the updated draft was being prepared for publication, the Home Office released two new reports, the Cantle Report and the Ministerial Group Report, which have raised significant points for the development of future public policy. This necessitated further updating to include a brief summary of these reports.

I hope the book presents the latest version available of many aspects of the story of struggle for racial justice in   Bradford and mirrors some similar images from elsewhere in Britain. I also hope that any failings in the policy and practice of race relations in the past may offer some lessons for working out improved measures to achieve the 2020 Vision and   ባ Bradford's current bid for European Capital of Culture 2008.

Ramindar Singh
May 2002

1

INTRODUCTION

Almost up to the end of 1960s, issues arising from the arrival in Britain of immigrants from the New Commonwealth countries were not perceived and discussed in terms of race-relations, racial justice or racial inequalities. For the white communities the major concern was to stop or at least to minimise and slow down the influx of black and Asian people into the country. They were also anxious to contain those already here within the inner city districts and to meet their needs with existing systems. For the immigrants themselves, the priority was to maintain jobs in the labour market, find living accommodation of any kind whatever and to get their families reunited. Despite some ups and downs in the labour market, they were able to find jobs and the availability of cheap old, often rundown properties provided them access to the housing market without any serious competition with local white people.

If there were any concerns about the relations between minority non-white groups and the majority white populations, these were generally expressed in terms of 'community relations'. The public sector and voluntary bodies set up to deal with these concerns were also referred to in those terms, for example, nationally the setting up of the Community Relations Commission and locally the emergence of community relations councils. Only by the mid-1970s were the issues of racial inequalities, racial discrimination, cultural diversity and race relations being widely recognised in terms of ''race' as a result of the minority communities steadily establishing their permanent roots in the country. At the political level, urgency in dealing with race related issues came in the early 1980s, largely as these became issues of social disorder with the recurrence of street riots from time to time.

Thus, race relations became a field of study in its own right with a complex set of concepts, such as, 'race', 'racism', 'race relations', 'community relations', 'integration', 'assimilation', 'pluralism', 'ethnic minority communities' or 'minority ethnic communities'. These terms were used to understand and interpret the contemporary reality of British society with the addition of new ethnic communities, and to provide objectives for social policy makers and for the action of custodians of social responsibility. There had been little long-term consensus on the precise meaning of these terms and they have been defined and redefined by politicians, political and social scientists over the last four decades.

A major contribution to the debate on the future of multi-ethnic Britain was the publication of the report of the commission established by the Runnymede Trust under the chairmanship of Lord Bhikhu Parekh. Part I of the Parekh Report (2000) examines a range of conceptual models of a vision for Britain. More recently (December 2001), in the wake of serious race riots in Oldham, Burnley and Bradford last summer, the publication of two reports by the Home Office, the Ministerial Group Report also called the Denham Report and the Ted Cantle Report, focus upon the concepts of 'Britishness', 'citizenship' and 'community cohesion'. It appears that community cohesion is becoming the governments' ultimate goal to achieve. The present study attempts to trace the progress of struggle for racial justice in Bradford, over a period of half a century, along the continuum starting with community relation, through race relations and multiculturalism, to community cohesion.

In order to present an accurate account of the local situation, in the present study, some of the key sociological terms are used in the same particular way as they have been used in the documents of the local institutions whose policies and approaches are examined here. For example, *'community relations'* means basically 'social interaction' between the non-white population and the local white population. *'Minority ethnic communities'* or 'ethnic minorities' refer to the people of Pakistani, Bangladeshi, Indian, African and Caribbean origin, to the exclusion of white ethnic communities. 'South Asians' refer to the people of Pakistani, Bangladeshi and Indian origin. The term *'race relations'* is used to encompass a comprehensive set of initiatives such as the fight against racism, direct as well as institutional; the curtailment of racial harassment in all shapes and forms; the development of equal opportunity policies; the measures designed to eliminate race

2

inequalities; and the steps taken to promote good relations between diverse local communities for peaceful co-existence. In essence, *'struggle for racial justice'* implies attempts to achieve an all-inclusive fair and just society.

A superficial view may suggest that the fundamental issues of race relations in Britain have not significantly changed. Their nature and magnitude may have altered but not much. The political nature of policies adopted so far to deal with racial prejudice, discrimination and inequalities keep on changing but their impact on reducing these social ills has been minimal and is less obvious. In fact, over the years, all minority ethnic groups in Bradford have made tremendous efforts to adjust themselves to the new economic and social environment in which they have set their roots permanently. In doing so some groups have been quicker and more successful than others. Some groups feel more at ease whilst others are still showing signs of constant worry and insecurity.

In dealing with contemporary race relations issues in Bradford, I believe, a study of the local history of race and community relations may offer some useful insights in understanding the present, anticipating the future and mobilising energy in the right directions for a change. With this objective in mind, the present publication provides a brief demographic picture of ethnic minority communities in Bradford and an account of the equal opportunity policies of Bradford Council. It contains a survey of some key events and 'agents of change' which have impacted on the race and diversity environment of the entire Bradford District. It also examines some of the factors that are likely to have a powerful impact in shaping future race relations in the District. A full life story of Bradford Racial Equality Council (BREC) is included so that lessons can be learnt from its achievements and its failures, lessons which should inform all those seeking to map a way forward for future race relation in the District.

The study does not claim to be a comprehensive survey of events or a full critical account of the achievements and failures of all local initiatives in the struggle for racial justice. However, it is intended to provide a benchmark and a stimulant for future work in the field to fill gaps and to amend any inaccuracies.

The struggle for racial justice

It is contended that the story of Bradford, however unique it may be, is likely to share many common features of experience with other cities with high concentration of minority ethnic communities. It is hoped that this work may stimulate interest in documenting an account of race relations in other cities that would assist in building up a bigger picture of the changes in race relations in Britain.

The life story of BREC is compiled largely from three sources: (a) minutes of the Council's Executive Committee, sub-groups and panels meetings, (b) Annual Reports presented to the full Council, and (c) my own recollection of the activities of BREC and its earlier versions. Memory can always fail and is generally selective. Formal minutes and reports of meetings of organisations are generally short and selective and usually written with a bias. These limitations have been compensated to some extent by comments from two past Directors and two former Chairs of the BREC on an earlier draft. Thus the account is as full and accurate as could be expected. However, any remaining omissions, inaccuracies and inadequacies are all mine, and mine alone.

Information on Bradford Council's policies is derived from various reports and council papers. The Telegraph & Argus has been the prime source for building up the broad picture of key events that have impacted on race relations in the city.

The account of race relations presented here is largely based on the documented material and the author's reflections on his personal experience of over 35 year active involvement in race relations locally, regionally and nationally; and his experience of teaching race relations as an academic. An alternative and complimentary perspective on local race relations could be the *'peoples' perspective'*, which is missing from this account. To record the peoples' perspective is highly desirable and would be most useful in determining objectives and direction for future race relations policy and other initiatives. The peoples' perspective can be obtained on similar lines as the work carried out by the Bradford Heritage Recording Unit in the 1980s. (1) In a limited way the recently

4

published Ouseley Report on the state of race relations in the District and the Cantle Report provide this perspective.

The reflections on the last fifty years struggle for racial justice cannot be summed up in more precise and simple words than those of Frances McNeil:

"For a long time the favourite self-image for Bradford was a place where everyone got on well despite their differences. The truth is that we largely ignore each other and get on with our lives until something goes wrong. There is a lot of segregation and separation in Bradford, but what emerges again and again is the sense of shared struggle". (2)

2

THE DEVELOPMENT OF RACE RELATIONS ORGANISATIONS IN BRITAIN

A Critical Overview

This chapter attempts to present an overview of the development of race relations bodies in Britain. It examines particularly the work of the local voluntary Community Relations Councils (CRCs) / Racial Equality Councils (RECs) and the national bodies, the Community Relations Commission and its successor Commission for Racial Equality, set up under the race relations legislation. To do so in relation to the study of one individual REC is important for three reasons: (a) Changes in the structure, role and activities of all CRCs / RECs reflected the changes in the duties and priorities of their national main funding bodies, that is, the two commissions. (b) Local CRCs/RECs to a large extent mirrored the problems faced by the national commissions. (c) The relations between the CRCs/RECs and the national commissions were not always of mutual respect, admiration, nor tension-free.

My experience at the Comission for Racial Equality (1988-92) and my close involvement in resolving the difficulties of the CRCs in the Calderdale and Kirklees districts convinced me about the common nature of the problems and issues facing the CRC/RECs across the board. It is hoped that even this brief understanding of the national scene would enable the reader to appreciate the work of the Bradford Racial Equality Council and the problems that it experienced in its life-time. Thus, it should be possible to make a realistic judgement about the contributions it made to the struggle for racial justice in the city.

The local voluntary organisations concerned with community relations and race related issues have been in existence from the early sixties under various names. Gradually, most of them named themselves as Community Relations Councils (CRCs). In 1990 most of the CRCs renamed themselves as Racial Equality Councils (RECs). The Community Relations Commission and since 1976 its successor, the Commission for Racial Equality (CRE), have been the regular source of CRCs / RECs' funds for staffing and key projects. Local authorities contribute towards their administrative costs and in many cases towards the salaries of some caseworkers.

The origin and development of community relations organisations are very closely related to the development of immigration and anti-discrimination legislation in Britain. With the introduction of the first Immigration Control Act 1962, a non-statutory body called the Commonwealth Immigrants Advisory Council (CIAC) was established at national level to advise the Home Office. At the local level some voluntary liaison committees and international friendship clubs were set up to help new immigrants in finding their way around. The churches took the lead or acted as patrons in the setting up of welfare associations for immigrants and friendship clubs and were later joined by black and white middle class people in the establishment of race and immigration related discussion forums. Political and official initiatives were slow to recognise the need for such voluntary organisations.

In 1965, with the establishment of the Race Relations Board, a government sponsored body, the National Committee for Commonwealth Immigrants (NCCI) replaced the CIAC at national level and the setting up of Voluntary Liaison Committees (VLCs) was encouraged in the areas of immigrant settlement. The1965 White Paper: *Immigration from the Commonwealth*, defined the work of the local liaison committees as providing "the necessary focal point in their areas for the co-ordination of effort and a channel for the exchange of information, ideas and experience. Above all they help to create a climate of mutual tolerance in which the stupidity of racial prejudice cannot survive". NCCI became a channel for providing funds for the appointment of local liaison officers by the VLCs. Broadly speaking VLCs worked on the principle of "information, education and welfare". They worked towards the integration of immigrants into white society, the elimination of racial prejudice through education and co-ordination of local efforts in creating a climate of mutual tolerance.

In 1968 the government established the Community Relations Commission (CRC), a statutory body with three main functions:

(a) to encourage and promote harmonious race-relations; help other organisations in this field and co-ordinate their work and efforts.

(b) to advise the Secretary of State on matters referred to it and on other matters which need attention.

(c) to educate and to carry out research in the field of race-relations.

The establishment of the Commission resulted in the name change of VLCs to Community Relations Committees (CRCs) and encouraged the CRCs to promote inter-racial harmony more ambitiously and elaborately, at the same time making their work more controversial. The CRCs were independent organisations run by executive committees annually elected by large general council memberships of individuals, local authority representatives and voluntary organisations. Other than the money for specific projects, the Commission and local authorities remained the providers of grants for the running of CRCs. Most of the local CRCs became umbrella organisations for ethnic minority associations. They also started campaigning against racial discrimination - the widespread existence of which was established through a number of research studies. The restrictive 1971 Immigration Act prompted CRCs on the one hand to campaign actively against the alleged "racist immigration policy" and on the other hand to handle immigration casework.

The Race Relations Act 1976 replaced the Community Relations Commission and the Race Relations Board by a new single organisation, the Commission for Racial Equality (CRE). The CRE became responsible for both "promotional" as well as "enforcement" roles. The CRE had the two main duties of:

(a) working towards the elimination of discrimination, and

(b) promoting equality of opportunity and good relations between persons of different racial groups generally.

At the local level CRCs working with the CRE became responsible for developing good race-relations, equality of opportunity and the elimination of racial discrimination. It was also recognised that CRCs should support ethnic minority organisations, local authorities and other organisations such as law centres in furthering the objectives of the CRE.

In practice the work of the CRCs varied extensively. Variations occurred for a variety of reasons. As the ethnic composition of minority communities differed from city to city it resulted in differences of approach depending on the nature and magnitude of the problems of the local immigrant groups. The differences in the experience, background and skills of local community relations officers (CROs) were strongly reflected in their activities and methods of working. Variations in the general political style of local communities impacted considerably upon different CRCs' approaches to community relations in particular towns and cities as the local authorities were major contributors to their funding. Some CRCs had better access to human and financial resources and were therefore, better placed to carry out a wide and varied range of activities. As the politics of race relations kept on changing new CRCs were adopting fresh and sometimes different approaches compared with the earlier established councils.

By remaining outside local authority structures CRCs were able to attract non-town hall grants and maintain their independence of view and action. At times it helped them to preserve their political independence and act as ethnic pressure groups.

Criticism of CRCs in the 1980s

During the 1980s some serious comments were made about the working and role of the CRCs. For example, it was argued that the presence of CRCs was designed to kill the development of independent 'civil rights' movements by co-opting leaders from the minority ethnic groups.

The Home Affairs Committee of the House of Commons claimed:

> *"it is wrong-to regard CRCs as the sole 'spokesman' body of the ethnic minority community.....In any event CRCs and CROs must recognise that public funding of voluntary bodies bears with it an obligation to perform in a way that is visibly in the public interest". (1)*

The Home Office (November 1981) *Report On Racial Attacks* stated:

The struggle for racial justice

"In the long term ..the aim of community organisations (CRCS) should rather be to encourage direct contact between the communities (ethnic minority) they serve and the authorities".

The Lord Scarman Report (1981) argued:
"Local CRCs are, or should be, at the centre of attempts to foster a harmonious, multi-racial society. Their primary duty is to foster harmony, not undermine it".

From the evidence given to the Scarman Inquiry it also emerged that some CRCs appear to have had a tendency to act purely as special interest lobbying for minority groups. Some were too readily influenced by extreme political views and many too often expected to be the sole channel of contact and communication between the ethnic minorities and official bodies. (2)

Right up to the end of the 1980s, the CRE and local RECs (and their earlier counterparts) shared common objectives and concerns, and were operationally mutually dependent. However, serious tensions between them were always evident. CRCs were critical of the Commission's bureaucratic approach, lack of political will to fight discrimination, slow and ineffective communication, and absence of genuine consultation with the grass roots. On the other hand, as the major provider of their funds, the CRE wanted an effective say in their work programme, appointment of staff and financial matters. CRCs were both critical of the Commission's inability to provide them with the right direction and focus for their activities and at the same time resistant to the CRE's attempts to set an agenda for them. Therefore, for a long time it was effectively a marriage of convenience.

Some CRCs were acting as purely campaigning bodies on race related issues. Many were concentrating on organising multi-cultural social events and doing casework relating to immigration, nationality and welfare benefits for members of minority communities. Their clients were almost exclusively blacks and Asians. Very few of them were actually pro-actively involved in combating racial discrimination.

Nevertheless, a small number of them were handling race discrimination casework.

Achieving an effective balance between the multiple roles they were trying to perform proved problematic. Questions were raised about the unbalanced ethnic composition of the CRCs' staff, their dogmatic approach and their professional capabilities.

Most CRCs became local power bases for their local black and Asian communities. Some became forums where minority communities drew comfort and cooperation from one another in dealing with their particular problems. Some became continuous battlefield between various ethnic groups, each trying to gain control. Such tensions made them self-absorbed and externally ineffective. Some CRCs regularly experienced serious conflicts between appointed staff and their elected officers. Some CRCs developed disagreements with their local authorities. In most cases, marginalised minority groups were complaining about under representation, and many faced actual or threats of boycott. Consequently, many CRCs lost public credibility.

In the wake of race riots in some major cities in the 1980s, indicating the poor state of race relations and racial inequalities, particularly in inner city areas, most local authorities established their own race relations units, appointed race advisers and equal opportunities officers. This development was seen as a potential threat to the very existence of CRCs. Some discontented CRC officers sought new career opportunities in the local authority sector. As a consequence of this development, local authorities felt a diminished need for the CRC staff to advise and liaise with minority ethnic communities. Some local authorities stopped funding their CRCs and many of those who continued funding did so mainly as a matter of political expediency.

Furthermore, the growth of ethnic minority organisations had more or less eroded the intermediary role of the CRCs. The emphasis from 'black' had considerably shifted to 'ethnic minorities' and 'ethnicity'. This posed serious difficulties for the CRCs in keeping a common focus for their activities. It became difficult for them to maintain a reasonable balance in dealing with the race issues affecting, culturally, religiously and linguistically diverse communities. Therefore, a cohesion and unanimity in their decisions became highly problematic, as did their claim to be a representative body for all minority groups.

CRCs as a movement was seen to have failed both to develop good race relations and to reduce racial disadvantage and inequality. In their present form they were seen as irrelevant.

Criticisms of the Commission for Racial Equality in the 1980s

1. The Commission was finding it extremely hard to shake off the widely held view of it as an organisation for, and representative of, the black and Asian population. This was a serious impediment in the CRE's way if it was to achieve its objectives.

2. The Commission consistently faced difficulties in achieving consensus among its staff about its mission and direction.

3. Equal opportunity policy within the Commission was one of the major internal problems. The Commission is expected to be a model equal opportunity employer, quite rightly so. Despite the implementation of rigorous procedures, it failed to achieve a representative distribution of ethnic groups within its workforce. For example, there were hardly any Chinese working within the CRE, South Asians were under-represented among the secretarial and administrative staff, only a handful of Sikhs worked within the staff, whilst black staff dominated the London office. The fifty per cent target set for women employees was never achieved. Black and Asian women were seriously under-represented at senior grades. There were accusations of discrimination against black and Asians in appointments, particularly in promotions to senior grades.

4. The younger generation of South Asian backgrounds did not show any particular interest in working for the Commission or in the race relations area at national level as a career. The physical location of the Commission near Victoria (London) had attracted mainly women of Afro-Caribbean background into junior civil service grades. Given these factors, it is surprising that the Commission did not set itself more realistic targets for women and ethnic minorities.

That the Commission suffered itself from internal tensions and divisions within its staff along ethnic lines is both instructive and salutary.

5. The Commission was criticised for being ineffective and too beauracratic from within and from outside.

6. The CRE was heavily criticised by leaders of Muslim communities for its failure to include religious discrimination among its recommendation for amendments to the RR Act 1976 in 1992.

7. It was accused of its insensitivity to Muslim issues and concerns particularly during the Rushdie Affair and its aftermath.

Reviews of CRCs / RECs in the 1990s

The work of RECs has been subject to periodic reviews. The National Association of Community Relations Councils, with funding from the CRE, commissioned a review and evaluation study of the CRCs by the Policy Studies Institute in 1986. A report by Gay and Young: *Community Relations Councils: Roles and Objectives* was published in 1988.

The report of the study resulted in a major shake up of the CRCs under the slogan, "New Partnership". The 'new partnership' attempted to make the local community relations movement more appropriate for the 1990s. The aims and objectives of the CRCs were re-defined and made more consistent with those of the REC. In many ways, the RECs started working almost as local branches of the CRE. However, it was acknowledged that they should and would maintain their voluntary and independent status. The partnership was based on equality of status. Most CRCs accepted changes but not without inhibition and pain.

Following the publication of the report the Commission developed its *"New Partnership for Racial Equality"*. The main components of the new partnership included all community relations councils:
   ♦ changing their names to Racial Equality Councils (RECs) to accurately reflect their collaborative working and joint planning relationship with the Commission.

13

♦ preparing annual programmes of work to have a better and sharper focus with output · measures and performance indicators and to concentrate on work in the areas of policy development, public education and community development as well as race discrimination and racial harassment casework.

♦ conforming to a new model constitution which was to offer them greater stability, stronger corporate management with executive functions exercised more collectively and with less tension between their representational and functional roles.

♦ using the opportunity to strengthen the local partnerships which should exist with local authorities and ethnic minority groups in tackling racial equality issues at a local level.

Since embarking on the *'New Partnership for Racial Equality'* in 1990 it is clear that many RECs do not see themselves as representing all ethnic minority communities in their localities, nor do many wish to act as a representative forum reflecting local opinion on race issues. Without such a commitment many questions arise about the scope, nature and purpose of the CRCs giving mixed views about the effectiveness of the *'New Partnership'*.

The latest review of the RECs was carried out by KPMG in 1996-97 for the CRE. In its report *A Fundamental Review of the Public Service Role of Racial Equality Councils* for the Commission for Racial Equality submitted in June 1997 it makes some interesting observations and recommendations:

• The report questions the potential benefits of the RECs adopting the position of not being "representative" of the wider community. It expresses the concern that "the credibility of RECs in local life and their degree of involvement in mainstream local issues" have been diminished as a result of this position in many areas.

• "Local public education and policy development work is increasingly important for RECs." Many RECs were working very effectively in partnership with other local agencies in local racial equality work.

- The report found: "that RECs were not closely enough integrated with the development of local authority community strategy or race policy." It also found "many RECs uncomfortable about combining their role of partner to local authorities whilst also needing to monitor them and their performance in specific areas which have direct racial equality implications."
- The report recognises the serious problems associated with the "system of lay member control" and the "local racial equality work being brought into disrepute by acrimonious disputes within RECs".
- The report recommends that gradually RECs should become more independent of the CRE in areas such as terms of constitution, electoral arrangements and terms of employment.

Conclusions

Given the relative small size of the Commission and the voluntary CRCs/RECs organisations, the continued lack of commitment of many senior politicians and the strong anti-ethnic attitudes of certain sections of the white population, their achievements over the years are not mean. It is unrealistic to measure their success, rather the lack of it, in terms of the persistence of racial discrimination, disadvantage, violence and harassment in Britain. They had been expected to take on an enormous task, a task with complex dimensions, but with limited support from the government and the population in general.

The criticisms of these bodies may well be worthy but there is one basic fact to be acknowledged and this is that Britains' race laws are stronger and the enforcement body the CRE is more powerful and effective than any similar organisation in Europe. The continuing high level of discrimination in many walks of life in Britain is sometimes used as evidence to justify the relative failure of the CRE. It is also an argument used by those who advocate that the Commission's law enforcement functions are largely redundant and it should confine its duties to education and exhortation (3)

Leon Hawthorne (4) argues that black underachievement, so much as it exists, has socio-economic causes. It is not simply a product of current racism or discrimination, but that of centuries ago. It is essentially

15

working class under-achievement. Therefore, the money spent on the CRE and other branches of the race industry, such as local RECs and race advisers in local authorities, should be directed to develop free enterprise and personal diligence in the black community.

Reflecting on the American experience some people argue that the race relations legislation and the activities of race relations organisations has only helped the black middle class whilst the majority of the blacks in Britain remain trapped in poor living and working conditions in the inner city ghettos. They argue that today's need is no longer civil rights as much as economic rights. Some argue that race relations laws should be scrapped because they do not benefit blacks and Asians in Britain, they are an affront to self-respecting blacks and are a stumbling block to black progress. Self-esteem has got to replace self-pity and discipline has got to take over moaning. Good functional education should replace liberal multi-cultural learning. (5)

The Home Office has worked closely with the CRE on the implementation of the Race Relations (Amendment) Act 2000 which came into force on 2 April 2001. The new legislation has outlawed racial discrimination in all public functions not covered by the original 1976 Act with some limited exceptions. The Home Secretary will also be bringing forward secondary legislation to impose specific duties to promote racial equality upon key public bodies. The CRE is expected to provide codes of practice to guide public authorities on how to fulfil their new statutory requirements. The public sector is expected to lead by example in achieving the Government's "wider vision--a vision of a successful multicultural Britain, where every citizen and every community earns and gives respect." (6) In the context of the changes in race relations legislation and the delivery of equality, the CRE is talking about 'new rules of engagement between local communities and the public services'. (7) However, it is not clear at this stage what changes may be introduced by the CRE in its own rules of engagement with the local level racial equality councils, if any.

3

MULTI-ETHNIC PORTRAIT OF BRADFORD

Bradford's contemporary ethnic portrait is a consequence of more than 150 years of immigration into the city. There have been four distinct groups of immigrants, Irish, European merchants, people from Central and Eastern European countries and New Commonwealth citizens in that chronological order. (1)

Irish

The earliest European immigrants to come to Bradford were the Irish whose numbers locally increased rapidly in the early decades of the nineteenth century. By 1901 there were 4294. (Richardson, 1976, P 95). After that date the Irish community was increasingly dominated by second and subsequent generations who were then characterised as indigenous. In the late 1960s the Catholic population in Bradford was estimated to be around 40,000. This may give an approximate idea of Irish ancestry in the city - although all Irish immigrants were not Catholic and not all Catholics were Irish.

The Irish immigration to Bradford was caused primarily by the economic opportunities offered in the locally expanding textile and other industries. Jobs were mostly low-paid and low-status. Besides this "pull" factor, over-population together with declining agricultural and textile employment sectors, "pushed" many Irish to leave their homeland. Textile manufacturers also directly recruited some Irish labour.

The Irish initially formed a distinct community which was driven by economic necessity to concentrate in a limited number of decaying inner-city areas such as White and Black Abbey, Wapping, Nelson Court and Adelaide Street. There they clung to their own distinctive cultural life-styles that were supported by the growth of Catholic churches and schools.

Initially there was considerable suspicion and hostility between the Irish and native Bradfordians. The assumptions about Irish wage cutting, cultural and linguistic differences, fear of popery, their drunkenness, immorality and criminality created local prejudice against them. The Irish also brought over to Bradford their own sectarian rivalries between Catholics and Orangemen. Eventually upward economic and social mobility among the Irish immigrants brought spatial dispersal, respectability and acceptance.

German Merchants

Martin Hertz, is believed to have been the first German immigrant, appearing in Bradford in 1820. He was the forerunner of a select but very influential group of German merchants who settled in the city. Most of them came from Northern Germany. Some were Protestants who built their still existing Evangelliche Kirche in Great Horton Road. But many of them were Jews, including Charles Semon, who became Mayor of Bradford in 1864. They numbered 65 in 1861. Many quickly became naturalised and some settled in such exclusive housing areas as Claremont, Manningham, and Heaton.

The German merchants contributed much to the economic development of Bradford between the 1840s and 1914. The upper class Germans remained influential and respected until the outbreak of war in 1914 when local xenophobia destroyed their assurance and they were seen as spies by the rest of the population. Besides opening up direct trade with Germany from their exotic warehouses in Little Germany, they encouraged technical developments in the woollen industry. Their contributions to the local economy as well as the social and cultural life of Bradford outweighed their fairly small numbers. Even today, Bradford celebrates their major landmarks in Little Germany. By the end of 1930, this distinctive community of merchant Jews had disappeared largely through assimilation into the local community.

From the 1880s the prosperous German Jews were joined by a small number of poorer Jews who were driven out of Tsarist Russia. They created their own culture centred on the Orthodox Synagogue in Spring Gardens, Manningham, separate and distinct from the Jewish Reform Synagogue in Bowland Street. The estimated number of Jewish families in Bradford in 1976 was between 400 and 500.

Eastern Europeans

The next phase of European immigration occurred as a direct result of the ending of World War Two with the absorption of such Eastern European countries and regions such as Estonia, Latvia, Lithuania, Poland and the Ukraine into the USSR. Many of these new immigrants had served in armies in the West during the war and others had become refugees in the wake of the advancing Red Army.

After 1945, because of labour shortages in this country, the post-war Labour Government recruited workers from European refugee camps and many of these recruits eventually settled permanently in the Bradford area. A small number of Italians also came to Bradford in the 1950s and 60s. The vast majority of these new immigrants were women coming to work in the textile mills. Bradford Heritage Recording Unit estimated that in 1987, the number of people who had their origin in Central and Eastern European countries was as follows: Poland 4,000; Ukraine 3,700; Italy 1,500; Yugoslavia 1,200; Estonia, Latvia, Hungary and Byelorussia 500 each; Lithuania and Austria 200 each; and Germany 150, (Jowitt and Perks, 1987, p.12).

These Eastern European immigrants created their own social and religious infrastructure and have remained distinct ethnic communities. They have established their own churches or church services, clubs and their own supplementary schools to maintain their linguistic and cultural traditions. Like their predecessors they have assisted the economic development of the city and added to the variety of cultural riches of Bradford.

The struggle for racial justice

Africans / Caribbeans

Migrants from a number of small islands in the Caribbean came to Bradford in the 1950s to work in the local industries and the health services. Nearly two thirds of them were from Dominica. The number in the city was always small. Currently, there are about 6,300 people of African and Caribbean origin in the city, forming 1.3 % of the total population. Initially, the majority of them lived in the Lumb Lane area of Manningham. Although they are now very thinly spread in all parts of Bradford, their main concentrations are in the Little Horton and University areas. The majority of the present Afro-Caribbean population is Bradford -born. They belong to various Christian denominations such as Catholics, Protestants, Seventh Day Adventists and Pentecostal churches. They are an extremely marginalised group in the city. They suffer equally from prejudice and discrimination in the labour market but have escaped being targeted by the media for being a problem or for racial harassment. In 1998 black workers constituted 1.4% of the labour force of working age in Bradford whilst their proportion in the total population of the city is 1.3 per cent.

South Asians (2)

The South Asian immigrants provided much needed cheap labour to the local textile and manufacturing industries in the post Second World War era. They helped to exploit spare capacity in these industries and hence increase their profitability, at least for a while. Some South Asians found work on the buses in the city. South Asians are a classic example of economic migrants. However, some non-economic factors have played a significant part in the processes of immigration from the Indian sub-continent. There is an old tradition of emigration from areas such as Punjab, Gujarat, Mirpur and Sylhet. People growing up in such 'emigration cultures' compete with one another for employment opportunities abroad. Sending people away from home is an indicator of economic success and enormous social pride for families within their own communities. A large number of South Asian people came as part of such a 'chain migration' phenomenon, that is, to join their families, friends and relatives. Some Asians came from East African countries, e.g. Kenya and Uganda, due to the insecurity caused by policies of 'Africanisation' in those countries.

A small-scale inflow of South Asian immigrants in the middle of the 1950s suddenly turned into an influx, particularly of Pakistani Muslims, partly to "beat the ban" in the form of the 1962 Immigration Act. Their number grew fast and a sizeable community was established very rapidly. Most of the families of Indian immigrants were reunited by the middle of the 1970s. However, it was with the tightening of immigration laws which gradually eroded the rights of the dependants of migrants to enter Britain, that most of the Pakistani and Bangladeshi immigrants decided to bring their families over. The primary immigration from the sub-continent ended almost three decades ago and even the family reunion stage has been over for all groups since the middle of 1980s. Nevertheless, a small number of people mainly from Bangladesh and Pakistan continue to come to Bradford as prospective marriage partners of children already born here.

According to the 1991 Census, there were 62,243 people of South Asian origin in the city. They formed 13.6%of the total population of Bradford. Since then the South Asian population of the city is estimated to have increased significantly.

The current estimated population of ethnic minority groups is as in the table below.

Ethnic Composition of Bradford District's Population
Year 2000

Ethnic Origin	Population	Percentage of Total Population
White	386,289	78.8
Pakistani	71,197	14.5
Indian	13,682	2.8
Black	6,313	1.3
Bangladeshi	5,670	1.2
Others	7,051	1.4
All Groups	490,102	100.0

Source: *Research Section, BDMC, Population Estimates in Bradford District, July 1997*

Ethnic minority groups (excluding Chinese) currently constitute 19.8 per cent of the total Bradford District's population. Almost the entire population of Pakistanis and Bangladeshi is Muslim. The people of Indian origin are divided almost equally between Hindus and Sikhs with a very small number of Muslims. Chinese are included among "Others" and are estimated to be less than one percent of the total population. African and Caribbeans are included under the general category 'Black'.

It is estimated that during the period 1996-2011the Pakistani population will increase by 71.7%, the Bangladeshi population will increase by 82.1%, the Indian population will increase by 13.3% and the African / Caribbean population will increase by 12.3% whilst the white population would actually decrease by 6 per cent. (Bradford Metro Council, 1996)

The settlement pattern of Asians in Bradford displays some interesting features. According to the 1991 Census, nearly two thirds of the total population of Asian origin are settled in four wards of the inner city area. For example, of the total population of University Ward and Bradford Moor Ward, 68.4 per cent and 49.5 per cent of the people, respectively, are of Asian ethnic origin. Similarly, almost one third of the population of Toller and Little Horton Wards are Asians. Within this geographically compact area, people from the same country and even the same district within their home countries have settled very close to each other. (Bradford Metro Council, 1993, p. 12) A serious consequence of this concentration is that once they are settled in deprived, poor and declining areas of the city with limited access to better residential accommodation, their deprivation and disadvantage is perpetuated and exacerbated. Particularly the Pakistani and Bangladeshi Muslim communities who have remained in the inner city areas appear to be in a vicious cycle of general deprivation. (Ratcliffe, 1996 and Bradford Congress, 1996) During the last decade or so many Indians have moved out of their earlier areas of residence to sub-urban or new housing developments. The residential movement within the Pakistani community is slow and is largely confined to slightly better accommodation in the inner city wards earlier occupied by Indians.

Percentage share of the Bradford labour force of working age
1998

Ethnic group	Percentage of total labour force	Percentage of total population
Indian	3.0	2.8
Pakistani	8.2	13.5
Bangladeshi	0.6	1.1
All groups	11.8	17.4

Source: *Table 65 in BMDC & Bradford & District TEC,*
Bradford & District Economic Profile Vol. 6

The significantly lower contribution of the Pakistani and Bangladeshi groups to the District's workforce is due to a larger proportion of their children being under the age of 16 and a much smaller proportion of Muslim women in the labour market. Even in the areas of optimum employment opportunities available in the city the overall unemployment rate for ethnic minority groups has been almost three times higher than that of the population in general. Among the ethnic minority groups Pakistani and Bangladeshi communities have suffered the most.

The employment structure of Asians has changed from the time of their arrival. The textiles and manufacturing industries in the city have declined and so have the job opportunities in local transport. Therefore, the younger and more qualified South Asians have sought employment in the expanding service industries in the private sector and some have joined the professions and local authority services. A good number of middle aged workers squeezed out from declining sectors who had accumulated some capital have become self-employed mainly in retailing, off-licence shops, taxis, restaurants and newspaper agencies. The economic success of some Asian enterprises is quite remarkable. Almost 200 small and big Asian restaurants and take away food outlets have earned Bradford the title 'Curry Capital of Britain'. A number of small manufacturing firms in textiles and clothing, motor vehicle repairs and construction companies have established their reputations in the city. There are hundreds of other service outlets catering to the specific needs of the Asian communities. These are the signs of a booming ethnic economy.

Cultural and Religious Characteristics of South Asian Communities

Indians have three main religious groups in Britain: Punjabi Sikhs, Punjabi and Gujarati Hindus, and Gujarati Muslims. Despite some fundamental differences in religious beliefs and ways of worship, Punjabi Sikhs and Punjabi Hindus share a common language, culture, festivals and many social customs. Members of the same family in these groups may have Hindu as well as Sikh names. In Bradford, Punjabi Hindus, small in numbers, are widely diffused in settlement amongst the Sikhs. Most of the time the two communities celebrate social and religious festivals together, as they usually did in India. Social interaction between Punjabi Sikhs and Gujarati Hindus, a larger group than the Punjabi Hindus in Britain, is very limited. Despite their common origin from India, their cultures, life styles, and community languages are different. They are also located physically separate from the areas of Sikh concentrations. On the whole, contact between the Sikh and the Gujarati community in the city has been limited and superficial

Punjabi Sikhs and Hindus and the majority of Punjabi Muslims in Bradford come from a similar cultural background, speak the same language, share some dress and dietary patterns. The general attitude of the Sikhs and Hindus towards Muslims is still very much coloured by the legacy of historical events. The partition of the Punjab in 1947, at the end of British rule in India, involved the transfer of populations between India and Pakistan, based on religion. It resulted in bloody religious riots in which thousands of people lost their lives, added a fresh dimension to the already historically antagonistic state of social relations between the Sikhs and Hindus on the one side and the Muslims on the other. For most of the Sikhs and Pakistani Muslims, living side by side in Bradford is a new experience.

In the earlier years of South Asian immigration into the city, the settlement pattern of the new comers showed little evidence of a religious divide. However, over the years, with the re-uniting of families, a significant separation has occurred in the physical location of these two communities. Sikhs have gradually moved out from their initial residential areas such as Thornbury, Laisterdyke, Bradford Moor and West Bowling, making room for Muslim families from the Manningham and Lumb Lane areas to move in. Now the spatial divide between the Muslim and the Sikh-Hindu communities is marked and evident. This spatial divide between these communities has very little influence on their mutual social relations in Bradford, as social mixing between them was always limited.

The relations between different South Asian communities have normally been harmonious. Even in potentially explosive situations, mutual respect and peace have been observed. During the last few years, some serious clashes between groups of young Hindus-Sikhs and Muslims in places like Southall, Slough, Isleworth and Birmingham have been reported in the media. Most of these incidents involved youngsters from local colleges of further education. However, no such incidents have so far happened in Bradford.

A closer examination of the development of Asian communities in the city suggests that in cultural, religious and social terms they are self-contained communities. Over the years they have established a large number of their own separate organisations and places of worship. The interaction between the various communities is very limited and generally superficial. Despite some continued tension between various communities, as discussed later, they have lived in peaceful co-existence. However, internal segmentation leads to tensions and conflicts within each individual community. A tremendous amount of political activity within the ever-growing number of South Asian organisations is also evident.

4

RIPPLES ON THE PEACE AND HARMONY

This chapter provides a brief account of some race or community relations related incidents in Bradford that affected the interaction between various local communities and had important consequences for the city's race relations policies and approaches.

The inter-community events which affect the relations between religious groups in the sub-continent generally influence the mutual relations between Muslim, Hindu and Sikh communities in the UK too. At times the relations between South Asian communities in Britain can be characterised as being Pakistani, Indian or Bangladeshi. Thus, inter-community relations usually have religious and/or national dimensions. Despite the fact that tensions remain between the three religious South Asian groups in the city, open serious conflicts have been rare. For instance, when India and Pakistan were at war in 1965 and in 1971 with India siding with East Pakistan when it sought independence from West Pakistan to become Bangladesh, despite the serious tension in the environment, no serious conflicts occurred in Bradford. However, such events have always pushed the three communities further apart.

A demonstration in support of Bradford 12
Photograph by kind permission of T&A, Bradford

Bradford 12 1981

On July 11, 1981, in the grounds of a nurses' home in Bradford, a number of Asian young men made 38 petrol bombs by filling milk bottles with petrol and rags to be used against an expected 'Skinhead' attack on Asians in the city. No skinheads actually arrived in Bradford but the 12 young men involved in making the bombs were arrested and charged. They were tried at Leeds Crown Court and were eventually acquitted. They admitted making the bombs and argued in their defence that the bombs were made for 'self-defence' to protect their community as they doubted the police's ability to deal with such an attack just as the police had proved inadequate in Southall.

The *Halal* Meat Issue 1984

In Bradford the local abattoir had a *halal* section for quite a while before *halal* meat became a public issue with Muslim parents' demand for *halal* meat provision for their children in schools. What was a dormant subject suddenly started getting headlines in the press and brought the Muslim community into the firing line - keeping the race relations environment in the city highly charged for quite some time. A decision by the Education Special Sub-committee to provide *halal* meat to Muslim children in schools was fiercely opposed by Animal Rights Movement campaigners. Before the heated, four hour debate on the *halal* issue in City Hall on 6 March 1984, 3000 Muslims peacefully demonstrated in the city centre in favour of the decision of the Education Sub-committee. They were also supported by Labour councillors Mohammed Ajeeb, Barry Thorne and Abdul Hameed and Conservative councillors Eric Pickles and Peter Gilmour. Muslim parents also withdrew their children from schools for a day to show the depth of their feelings on the issue. The Council upheld the decision of its Sub-committee.

Councillor Norman Free, the Lord Mayor, commented negatively on the decision of the Sub-committee and thus broke the tradition of maintaining the neutrality of his official position. The highly controversial nature of the decision resulted in a few casualties in the next local elections. A major political casualty of the *halal* decision was Peter Gilmour, Keighley North's Conservative councillor, a staunch supporter of the Council's race relations policy, who lost his seat to the Labour candidate.

27

The *halal* issue in Bradford suddenly elevated the local Muslims' status as national leaders for Muslim causes. They learnt their first major lesson in how to use the media successfully to fight for their rights. This newly acquired skill was very shrewdly used by the Muslim community in the *Honeyford episode* that followed the *halal saga*.

Sikh Turban Campaigns

The Sikhs' campaign for the right to wear turbans started in 1965 in Wolverhampton and Manchester where the local bus companies refused to employ turbaned Sikhs. After a hard and prolonged campaign involving large demonstrations in all the cities of Sikh concentration, with one of the leading campaigners fasting unto death and threatening to commit suicide by pouring petrol over himself, Sikhs eventually won the right to wear turbans as a part of the uniform. The turban issue emerged once again, when a headmaster in the Midlands refused to allow a Sikh pupil to wear his turban to school. It resulted in a nation-wide campaign and eventually the case was taken to the Lords and won (Mandla v Dowell Lee, House of Lords, 1983)

A Sikh bus driver in Bradford.
Photograph by kind permission of Tim Smith

The T& A (6 October 1966) responding to the turban issue on the buses, commented: "if a man feels so strongly about the turban he should remain in the community where his views are shared". Following the successful ending of the national campaign, in Bradford the first turbaned Sikh conductor was appointed in November 1968. In August 1980 the turban issue captured the headlines in the T & A when the Mother's Pride Bakery refused to allow a Sikh employee to wear a turban. The dispute was resolved by negotiation and avoided public demonstrations.

The Sikhs had to fight equally hard, all over again, to win exemption from wearing crash helmets over their turbans when riding motorcycles (Motor-Cycle Crash Helmets (Religious Exemptions) Act 1976). More recently, the Employment Act 1989 (Section 11) has exempted turban-wearing Sikhs from any legal requirement to wear a safety helmet on a construction site. Despite the presence of a number of Sikhs employed in the building trade in the city it has never become a real issue. Overall, the turban issue touched Bradford only marginally.

The Blue Star Operation- Amritsar 1984

For the most part, there has been no serious religious antagonism between Sikhs and Hindus in the city. They have lived together in complete harmony. Nevertheless, the political events in the Punjab have always affected relations between the two groups. For example, the relations between the two communities in Britain became very tense and fragile during the Eighties after the 1984 events in India. In 1984, the Indian army's attack (the Blue Star Operation') on the Golden Temple in Amritsar (the holiest shrine of the Sikhs) seriously strained Hindu-Sikh relations in Britain. Again the assassination of the Indian Prime Minister, Mrs Indira Gandhi, by her Sikh bodyguards caused a wave of mass killings of Sikhs in some Indian cities. This outraged Sikhs the world over. These two incidents and the political movement for the creation of 'Khalistan' in the Punjab resulted in some youth militancy in Britain as elsewhere in the Sikh Diaspora. These events dented the generally harmonious Sikh-Hindu relationship for over a decade. Although no serious incidents of hostility occurred in Bradford, very strong anti-Hindu and anti-Indian Government feelings were publicly expressed by the Sikhs in the city as elsewhere in the country. In August 1984, members of the Bradford branch of the International Sikh Youth Federation organised a big protest demonstration and picketed the weekend long International Conference of Hindus in the city, organised by the Vishwa Hindu Parishad. However serious clashes were avoided.

29

The struggle for racial justice

Despite these severe tensions between the two communities formal relations between them did not completely break down. These incidents had little impact on the relations between the Sikhs and the white communities in the city.

CRC Elections 1987
The CRC elections in 1987 saw a big change in its Executive Committee. The reins of the CRC came into the hands of a team of young South Asians, who were suspected of gaining their majority in the Executive Committee through a pre-planned scheme described as a black power plot by the T&A. Most of them were believed to be members of the Black Workers Collective, an organisation operating among the Council employees. They were accused of having a "hidden agenda".

After the election Mohammed Ajeeb predicted that the CRC would die a natural death within three years. He contended that it had become a "black pressure group", whilst it was intended to be "a forum for discussion between different community groups". (T&A, 13 July 1978) The religious umbrella organisations of Sikhs, Hindus and Muslims threatened to withdraw their representatives as they were also concerned about the manner in which the annual election was conducted. The Bradford Council for Mosques, the Jamiyat Tabligh-ul-Islam mosque group of Southfield Square and the Azad Kashmir Association actually cancelled their membership of the CRC in July 1987.

The criticism surrounding the control and role of the CRC occupied many column inches in the T & A in the months of June and July 1987. The use of phrases such as "race relations industry" and "race relations mafia" became common currency in the media. There were two opposing views on local race relations policy. (a) The young black activists believed that the "City Hall race relations policies were run by toothless tiger bodies" and had no chance of fighting racial discrimination and harassment. (b) Mohammed Ajeeb argued that "a confrontational approach did not always work". Sian James, a T&A reporter, explored the background to these two views under the heading "Battle lines in Civil War. (T & A, 27 June 1987) It appeared that

30

Councillor Abdul Hameed, the deposed Chairman of the CRC and Ishtiaq Ahmed, the newly elected, politically shrewd and articulate chairman of the CRC, headed this civil war on one side. And, on the other side, it was lead by Mohammed Ajeeb, an older Labour Party statesman and chairman of the Council's RRAG.

The Gulf War Crisis 1990

During the 1990 Gulf Crisis, British and American forces were sent into Saudi Arabia to protect her from an attack by the forces of President Saddam Hussain of Iraq. Some British Muslim organisations including the Bradford Council for Mosques demanded withdrawal of British and American forces from Saudi Arabia, the holy-land of the Muslims. In doing this, British Muslims appeared to be challenging a political decision made by the British Government.

A national Muslim conference on the Gulf was held in Bradford on 20 January 1991. The first among the seven resolutions passed at the conference read: "The Muslim community of the U.K. is outraged at the savage destructive war waged by the U.S.A., Britain and their allies against the Muslims of Iraq."

The Bradford Council for Mosques also issued a press statement on 13 February 1991 that read:

> "The Muslim community is deeply outraged by the western aggression against innocent Muslim civilians in Iraq. It holds the British Government and those elements who have declared it a just war, as being jointly responsible for the massacre on 13th February, 91. The peoples of Islam are committed to both peace and justice. These deaths must therefore be avenged in accordance with Islamic law in due course.
> The house of Islam is at war with all those who attack its interest including those so called Muslims who are in fact fellow conspirators with the forces of western imperialism."

Once again, Bradford became centre stage of the crisis when Sher Azam and Liaquat Hussain, both leaders of the Bradford Council for Mosques, joined a seven-member delegation: "UK Islamic Mission to Iraq". Yet

The struggle for racial justice

again the Gulf War situation raised serious concerns about the 'loyalty' of British Muslims.

The Gulf crisis increased tensions in Bradford and attracted much anti-Muslim comment in the media. People were saying "Where does your loyalty lie, with our lads or with Muslim dictators"? It almost became a 'second cricket test' of the Norman Tebbit type, which suggested that Asians supporting Asian teams were somehow anti-British. The crisis increased the fragility of race relations in the city even further.

The Muslim Parliament, 1991

The establishment of a Muslim Parliament in Britain in 1991 again questioned the loyalty of British Muslims. This was understood to be promoting the notion that Muslims should be treated as a separate community subject to their own code of domestic law. The speeches of Dr. Kalim Siddique, the main force behind its establishment, raised serious concerns in the British media about the integration of British Muslims into mainstream British institutions. He vehemently argued against Muslims' integration into what he referred to as the 'corrupt bog land of Western culture'.

Muslim leaders in Bradford distanced themselves from the whole concept of setting up any such parliament. They characterised it as an unnecessary and divisive diversion from the critical issues facing British Muslim communities. Liaquat Hussain, President of the Bradford Council for Mosques, was scathing in his remarks about the Muslim Parliament and condemned it for being "undemocratic and deploying tactics that alienate the majority British people to Muslim grievances". He called it a "cruel joke with Muslim community and had no future". (New Statesman & Society, 10 January 1992)

Babri Mosque Demolition –Ayodhia 1992

The demolition of the Babri Mosque in Ayodhyia (India) in December 1992 by a group of militant Hindus created tension between the Hindu and Muslim populations of the city. Following attacks on Hindu temples by some Muslim youths in various British cities, it was reported that Hindu temples in Leeds Road and Little Horton Road were maliciously

32

attacked too. A meeting of the Bishop of Bradford with Hindu, Sikh and Muslim community leaders was organised to calm down the situation in the city. Police were requested to keep a watchful eye on Hindu community buildings.

The ongoing issue of Kashmir is another source of latent tension between the Hindu and Muslim communities in Bradford with the majority of its Muslim population originating from the 'Azad Kashmir' area of Pakistan. When four Muslim labour councillors in Bradford issued a statement on the emotive issue of freedom for Kashmir in February 1990, they attracted strong protests from the Vishwa Hindu Parishad and the Hindu Cultural Society of Leeds Road. They were accused of causing damage to Hindu-Muslim relations in the city.

A number of small incidents of damage to Hindu properties have revealed latent tensions between the two communities. For example, it has been alleged that Diwali lights in the city have been damaged by Muslim militant youths in 1996 and again in November 2000.

5

The Honeyford Affair

The Honeyford Affair 1984

Bradford had just thwarted the Muslim Parents' Association's bid in 1983 to take over five schools (including Drummond Middle School) from the LEA. It was still facing fairly overt resistance to its policy of compulsory Race Awareness Training (RAT) for its officers and elected members. Concerns over the Council's decision on the highly controversial *halal* issue were still vibrating when the *Honeyford affair* hit the city in a big way. Ray Honeyford had been appointed head teacher of Drummond Middle School in Manningham in 1980. The school had over 500 children and almost 90 per cent were of South Asian origin and nearly all of these were Muslim.

The *Honeyford affair* began in a confused way, its development was rapid and complex and its consequences became extremely significant for race relations in Bradford. It had three distinct aspects which all tangled together as the issue developed.

(a) Mr Honeyford displayed a strong dislike of some practices prevalent within the South Asian communities. *Firstly*, he was strongly opposed to the practice of Muslim parents taking their children to Pakistan on long visits particularly during school term times. He believed this practice was undesirable and seriously detrimental to the education of children. *Secondly*, he was critical of the tradition of severe physical punishment being administered on young children attending 'mosque schools'. In 1983, he reported the case of some children from his school being cruelly beaten by imams to the police. This provoked serious antagonism from some parents and the leaders of the Muslim community. *Thirdly*, his damning description of Pakistan in his published articles further deepened the feelings of Muslims in the Manningham area against him.

(b) Mr Honeyford was lukewarm in his support of Bradford Council's race relations policy and, furthermore, he argued that its concept of multi-cultural education was profoundly flawed. He firmly believed that the introduction of multi-cultural education policies offered little educational benefit to ethnic minority children whilst making white children a 'disadvantaged minority' in his own school. He was highly critical of the compulsory requirements of RAT for all those involved in recruitment and selection of staff, the contents of these training courses and the manner in which they were delivered. Bradford Council's race trainers refused to train him, citing his deep-rooted "racist attitudes".

(c) He was regularly publishing articles on the inherent weaknesses of multi-cultural education and making criticism of Pakistan and the Pakistani community in the city. It was *The Yorkshire Post* that produced a summary of Honeyford's article *"Education and Race-An Alternative View"* published in the little known New Right's journal, *the Salisbury Review*. Public knowledge of the article widened the circle of his opponents. His further articles that appeared in the Times Educational Supplement in September 1982 and September 1983, in the Salisbury Review of January 1984, a letter in the T&A, and an article in The Times, deepened the controversy about his position as a head teacher in a multi-cultural school and created more enemies for him.

On his side, Honeyford had the support of those who advocated an individual's right to "free speech".

Initially a small group of people including Sher Azam of the Council for Mosques, Marsha Singh of the Education Department (now an MP) and Tim Whitfield, then Senior Community Relations Officer, and Jenny Woodward met with some parents to discuss their concerns about Honeyford. The group decided to set up the Drummond Parents' Action Committee (DPAC) and elected Jenny Woodward its chair-person. The DPCA informed parents about the contents of Honeyford's writings, extracts from which were translated into Urdu and organised a campaign against his suitability as head teacher in Drummond School. It arranged for regular pickets at the school gate. It advised parents and other residents in the area to send letters of protest to the Education

Committee to demonstrate their condemnation of his views and to ask the school's governors to dismiss Honeyford immediately.

The conflict dragged on for two years. It took shape as a triangular fight: DPAC versus Honeyford, DPCA versus Bradford Council and Honeyford versus the Council. DPAC was exerting parental pressure on Honeyford to go by its action of continuous picketing at the school gate. It also managed on one occasion to withdraw children from the school and set up an alternative school in the nearby Pakistan Centre. At the same time, DPAC was putting pressure on the Education Committee for the dismissal of Mr. Honeyford on three counts: that he had lost the confidence of the children's parents, was an unsuitable head to run a multi-racial school and was against the Council's policy of multi-cultural education. In addition to such direct pressure on the Council, the heightened activities of DPCA became a potential danger to race harmony in the area. This danger was becoming more potent as the Education Department's indecisive, slow and protracted approach was polarising views on both sides.

The saga continued while the school was inspected by the LEA's education advisors/ inspectors. Mr Honeyford was suspended from his position; he challenged the suspension in the courts, and, eventually, resigned from his positon having negotiated a hefty financial deal with the LEA.

The political consequences of the Honeyford and *halal* affairs were writ large in the 1986 local election results. A major turn-out of Asian voters won Heaton Ward for the Labour Party and increased their majority in the Toller Ward. The Liberal Party lost Baildon, their traditional stronghold, to the Conservatives as their leader, Kathleen Greenwood, had voted for the removal of Mr. Honeyford. The Conservatives made a big issue of what they regarded as the 'over-concentration of resources' in the inner areas of Bradford and argued for a drift of resources to the 'outer areas'. Later attempts were made to remove Councillor Norman Free from the Labour party.

Three local Conservative MPs, Geoff Lawler, Marcus Fox, and Gary Waller, all claimed that Mr. Honeyford was "hounded out by extremists" whilst the Labour MPs Max Madden and Tom Torney were concerned about the "size of the bill for rate payers" and the damage caused to the "education of children and to race relations".

Racial attacks and incidents of racial harassment increased during and in the aftermath of the Honeyford affair and so did the warnings from the Workers Against Racism, a splinter group of the Revolutionary Communist Party. (T&A, 25 March 1986) The Bangladesh Youth Organisation said "They were also planning to set up self-help vigilante groups to deal with racist incidents in the area. Our aim is to help the police and not ourselves getting involved in violence". (T&A, 25 April 1984)

The *Honeyford affair* in the 1980s clearly demonstrated that white politicians sympathetic to South Asian issues had problems when trying to lead South Asian groups in their fight for equality and racial justice. It appeared that South Asians suspected their sincerity, and their own white colleagues rejected and ignored them as political opportunists. It also revealed that how poorly the views of South Asian communities were represented in the press.

During the period of the *Honeyford affair* Chris Perry, a supply teacher, prepared a dossier of racial incidents at Wyke Manor School and alleged racist remarks by staff against the school's black headmaster, Carlton Duncan. The pupils at the school staged a walk out.

Both the *halal* and Honeyford issues projected an image of Bradford that was first and foremost a city of Muslim immigrants, ignoring the fact that Hindus, Sikhs and African-Caribbean communities formed a substantial proportion of the local ethnic minority population. Furthermore, Bradford was portrayed as a city of conflict, always on the brink of explosion.

A serious impact on the Council's race relations policy came with the call from the RRAG chief, Mohammed Ajeeb, for the abolition of the race trainers who had hit the headlines during the Honeyford affair for branding him a 'racist'. He argued for the RAT to be made an integral part of general training courses and not an isolated, tagged-on training exercise. (T&A 21 June 1986) The training courses allegedly followed a "hidden agenda" and were "a brain washing exercise". The controversy about the role of Bradford Council's race trainers and its racism awareness training courses ended the six year old political consensus on race relations policy.

A poster printed in Urdu with the heading: Kick Out Honeyford

ہنی فورڈ کو نکالو !

بروز جمعرات 6 نومبر کاروائی کا دن

6

SALMAN RUSHDIE AFFAIR

When Salman Rushdie's novel, *The Satanic Verses*, was published in 1988 British Muslims demanded a ban on the sale of the book and burnt copies in public, first in Oldham and then in Bradford on 14 January 1989. Some of the street demonstrations against the book resulted in violent incidents. Two chief concerns emerged during the debate on these events. *Firstly,* that banning the sale and publication of a book amounted to denying an individual citizen the 'right of free speech', the most cherished principle of the western democratic system. Therefore, demanding a ban on the book by Muslims was seen as being " un-British". *Secondly,* Muslim support for the *'fatwa'* issued by the late Ayatollah Khomeini of Iran, pronouncing the death sentence upon Salman Rushdie, was interpreted as disloyalty to the British legal system as it amounted to a very public threat by a foreign country to execute a British Citizen.

Bradford remained under the spotlight of international media attention during the whole Rushdie affair. There were some large and violent public demonstrations by Muslims in the city against the book with the Bradford Council for Mosques playing a leading role in the campaign. They sought a change in the blasphemy law. Two leaders of the Bradford Council for Mosques, Faqir Mohammed and Sayed Abdul Quddus, were quoted as having backed the call for the death of the author. (T&A, 15 February 1989) However, the next day the Council issued a statement that their two officials had been "seriously misquoted". The statement emphasised that "the Council for Mosques does not support violence and is not inciting Muslims to break the law in the country in which they live".

Political opinion on the banning of the book became highly controversial. There was general support for the Muslims' right to protest but not for the manner in which the protest was being made. Despite his support for the Muslims' feelings of deep hurt, the Bishop of Bradford, the Right Reverend Robert Williamson, expressed his

The struggle for racial justice

anxieties about the serious damage the demonstrations might do to the city's race relations. However, he did not favour banning the book. Under pressure and threats from the Muslims local book shops and the public library took their copies off their open shelves and made them available only when asked for.

Rally calling for the banning of *The Satanic Verses* outside the Bradford City Hall
Photograph by kind permission of Tim Smith

On Saturday, 17 June 1989 a demonstration of almost 3000 protesters took place in the city centre. For the most part it was an amazingly peaceful march with banners highlighting the anger and frustration of the Muslim community over the lack of action on a ban and resistance to legislation protecting other religions from blasphemous acts. Somehow, a rowdy mob of 400 youngsters was led away from the main demonstration causing mayhem. Police in riot gear and mounted on horses tried to control the crowd. The mob frightened shoppers in city centre streets and left a serious trail of damage to properties. The protest ended in over 50 arrests.

It was the *Salman Rushdie affair* that made the Bradford Council for Mosques a political force not only locally and nationally but internationally too. Three people associated with the Council, Sher Azam, president of the Council, Ishtiaq Ahmed and Dr Shabir Akhtar, were repeatedly quoted by the press on the Rushdie situation. Whilst Dr

40

Akhtar presented the case against the book in a shrewd intellectual manner, Mr Azam and Mr Ahmed came over as moderate voices and peace-makers. Fortunately, their efforts kept the Islamic fundamentalists away from highjacking the issue for their own narrow interests. They successfully kept the *Islamic jihad* (holy war) off the streets of Bradford where it could have isolated and alienated Muslims in the city. The Council's position on the Rushdie affair was: "we reject the *fatwa* but defend the book-burning as having been a necessary attempt to communicate Muslim frustration and anger". Despite this relatively moderate position, the Council continued to receive highly abusive hate mail for a long time, its office was repeatedly attacked and its statements condemned.

One consequence, the way the Muslim leaders in the city saw it, was that "white reactions to their anger over Rushdie have exposed inconsistency, hypocrisy and prejudice within our multi-cultural but unequal society". Muslim leaders were saying openly that Bradford never had good race relations. They claimed that whenever they had asked for their rights in the past, they met with hostility and latent deep prejudice and racism coming to the surface. They frequently quoted the *halal* meat and Honeyford issues as examples. The Rushdie affair became a hot potato for local politicians such as Eric Pickles, leader of the Conservative Group in control of Bradford Council. The Bradford Council for Mosques asked its members to withdraw their support from all local MPs and councillors who were not ready to back its demands for the banning of the book and for extending the blasphemy law to include Islam.

It looked at the time as though all the good work of the 1980s was undone. Racial attacks in the city increased. White school children in the city were chanting "Rushdie our hero...Rushdie rules OK." In some areas of Bradford, Muslim youngsters felt the need to set up small vigilante groups to defend themselves from attacks by NF or BNP incited white youths.

The *Rushdie affair* highlighted the urgent necessity of defining the concepts of 'Britishness' and 'Multi-cultural Britain'. In a public letter written to a number of leading British Muslim organisations in Britain on 4 July 1989 John Patten, clarified the then Conservative

Government's position "*On Being British*". He stressed in his letter that there was "room for diversity and differences", he rejected "assimilation" and advocated "integration" or "active participation in the mainstream". He emphasised that:

> "*But the philosophy of integration or active participation in the mainstream also requires that we recognise and support those things which, by virtue of living in Britain, are common to us all. Those include: the framework of laws, freedoms, rights and obligations which we live under; the English language; and British history. One cannot be British on one's own exclusive terms or on a selective basis, nor is there room for dual loyalties where these loyalties openly contradict one another*"

Douglas Hurd in his *The Third 1989 Westminster Lecture* to the Tory Reform Group at St Stephens Constitutional Club, London (delivered on 16 May 1989) articulated his government's commitment to a 'multi-cultural Britain'. He stated that "*close to the heart of our philosophy lies the idea of respect for diversity in unity, of one harmonious but not homogenised nation*". He also stressed that:

> "*It is nonsense to claim that diverse cultural traditions of our minorities cannot be reconciled with loyalty to Britain and full participation in the life of this kingdom..... Our programme for action, as a Government and as a Party, must begin with commitment to equality of opportunity and uncompromising opposition to racial discrimination in whatever form it comes*".

7

MANNINGHAM RIOTS 1995 AND
STREET DISTURBANCES

West Bowling Disturbances 1989

Since the middle of the 1980s Asian youths had been involved in street disturbances on a number of occasions. For example, 130 Muslim youths armed with iron bars, rods and cricket bats were involved in an incident in West Bowling in July 1989. The rioters claimed that they were protecting their neighbourhood from a gang of drunken white youths because the police had failed to do so. (The Guardian,11 July 1989). During the incident the police were stoned and cars and other property damaged. The racial tension was believed to have been caused by the Muslim campaign against *The Satanic Verses*.

Manningham Riots 1995

Bradford was completely shocked by its first major disturbance in the Mannigham area of the city. The media described these street riots on the weekend of 9 to 11 June 1995 as 'race riots'. For two consecutive nights buildings were petrol bombed, cars were burnt, shop and pub windows were smashed, and a looting spree continued. A mile-long stretch of shops was destroyed with damage estimated at about a million pounds. Burning barricades were erected across a busy road and a crowd laid siege to the police station. Almost 100 police officers were involved and nearly a dozen youths were arrested. The events shattered the popularly held belief that Bradford was a city of 'harmonious community relation'.

The trouble was started when a police patrol tried to disperse a rowdy group of youths. The police were mocked and their car kicked by the youngsters as they ran off. Officers gave chase and tried to arrest some youngsters who had entered a house. Whilst arresting one youngster in the house the police were accused of physically pushing away a woman with a baby. This was viewed as damaging the 'honour of a Muslim woman' and became the central issue for the family concerned and for the entire Muslim community. However, claims and counter claims about the facts of the incidents lasted over the whole weekend.

The Telegraph & Argus carried comments and details of the incident for almost a week and the national media gave comprehensive coverage. Cries came from all directions 'to heal the wounds caused' and for the 'rebuilding of the shattered image' of good race relations in the city. Leaders of all communities and local politicians were involved in trying to cool down the situation. Bradford Council and local MPs called upon the Home Secretary to establish an independent public inquiry; but he turned it down.

There was a good deal of media speculation on the reasons for the riots. At the political level white local councillors called it 'simple lawlessness' and the Asian councillors blamed it on the police's 'aggressive and insensitive' handling of a delicate situation.

Most press reports described these riots as a manifestation of 'Muslim youth alienated within western culture'. They argued that the children of Muslim parents who were neither wholly westernised nor totally dissociated from Muslim values, were living in 'two worlds'. The weakening of traditional Muslim cultural and religious values and parental control was interacting with the fast growing influences of western standards and values. This also meant that the community had lost influence and control over the actions of its youth. The youngsters had lost respect for traditional community leaders, who, they argued, had paid little attention to their problems. Thus, these riots were part of a challenge to the authority of these leaders.

The riots were also linked to the disproportionate levels of unemployment, poverty, and general deprivation amongst the Pakistani and Bangladeshi Muslim communities living in the Manningham area as discussed in chapter 17. All these factors have contributed, directly or indirectly, to the mayhem.

Two significant features of these incidents emerged: (a) that only young Muslim males were involved and no Hindu or Sikh youth took part in the incidents; (b) only white and Indian owned businesses were among those attacked. Thus to call these street disturbances 'race riots' was clearly a misleading media description.

The Manningham riots conveyed some fairly clear messages about the position of Muslim youth in Bradford. It was evident that the street action was a result of the politicisation of Muslim youth through their participation in the earlier incidents during the Rushdie and Gulf war affairs. The youths had a heightened awareness of their civil and political rights compared to their parents. They had become more assertive with an obvious change in their strategies for dealing with their grievances. The disturbances occurred soon after the Muslims' strong public reaction to the ITV's *Band of Gold* series which depicted the gritty and sordid prostitution trade in the Lumb Lane area of Manningham. The vigilante groups that Muslims formed to push the prostitutes out of that area, almost unhindered by the police, achieved a very visible result. This sudden and recent taste for street power was demonstrated once again in the riots.

Bonfire Night Disturbances November 1998

Asian Muslim youth once again created serious disturbances in the Manningham area on Bonfire Night. The trouble started from the same spot in Garfield Avenue as the riots of 1995. A rampaging mob of some 80 youths set a garage on fire, destroyed a telephone box, burnt down a two-storey bargain shop, and torched a number of cars in nearby side streets. A barrage of missiles was targeted at police officers and the Lowcroft House police station. Repeated clashes occurred between a large contingent of police in riot gear and the youth. The incident was described as 'mayhem by a minority' and was condemned by local community leaders.

8

THE BRADFORD COMMISSION REPORT

The Bradford Commission Report

The Report of an inquiry into the wider implications of public disorders in Bradford which occurred on 9,10,11 June 1995

November 1996

The Bradford Congress appointed a voluntary commission in June 1995 to investigate the riots in Manningham. The Commission was chaired by John Barratt, a retired solicitor and former deputy Town Clerk of Bradford, Professor Sheila Allen, University of Bradford, and Mohammed Taj, a local trade unionist. Alan Sykes, acted as secretary and legal adviser to the Commission and Mrs Elaine Applebee facilitated the arrangements for the Commission meetings and collection of evidence. The Commission published its 213 pages long report on 20 November 1996.

The report had a very mixed reception. It received almost entirely negative reactions from Muslim community leaders and commentators. No reaction at all from Hindu and Sikh community leaders, perhaps they were not expected to comment as it was only Muslim youth involved in the riots. The commissioners were criticised mainly for making no firm recommendations and for not fixing the blame entirely on the police. One of the commissioners, Mr Taj, did not sign the main report and instead issued his separate alternative report. Partly for the same reasons as above. Furthermore, he contended that the main report did not highlight the failings of the Asian community clearly and strongly enough and had also ignored some of the significant evidence presented to the Commission.

In fact the report is a far more important and valuable document than the quick off the cuff reactions would suggest. It presented a sound, critical and fairly comprehensive analysis of the state of race relations in the city. It examined in some detail a number of highly complex, sensitive and long-standing issues that the politicians and community had often refused to publicly admit. The report was right in suggesting that "there are no quick-fix solutions" to some of these issues. The blunt conclusion of the report as summarised by the T&A (21 November 1996) was: "A lack of vision. A lack of direction. A lack of strategy. A lack of focus". The report contains food for serious thought and is vital reading not only for understanding the reasons for the Manningham riots in summer 1995 but for developing a vision of race relations in the city for a long time to come.

A number of major institutions in the city developed their own responses to the Commission report. Sadly, the responses of most institutions were nicely worded statements of 'good intentions to work towards the elimination of racial discrimination and racial disadvantage unsupported by firm action plans with time-scaled targets and a commitment to monitoring results. Some institutions, including Bradford College and the University of Bradford, took this wonderful occasion to publicise how much they had already done, however, without any evidence to support the level of success of their previous initiatives. Others like the Chamber of Commerce and Bradford Racial Equality Council thought it would be an appropriate opportunity to set an agenda for action by other people. The police were quick to announce the appointment of a few more 'community affairs officers' and to push their campaign to recruit more officers from minority ethnic communities.

Bradford Council's "Response to the Bradford Commission Reports" released on 25th March 1997 was 43 pages long. The document was full of explanations of Council strategies, action plans with very clearly marked implementation and achievement dates. The Council displayed a clear understanding that its responses would be judged by the results achieved.

> "The Council fully accepts that in the event, it will be judged by what it does, not by what it says, which is why this report has avoided vision statements and gone for concrete proposals, with targets and time-scales." (p. 43)

The struggle for racial justice

However, it qualified its commitment by providing no firm guarantee for the full implementation of their proposals.

> *"We believe the proposals are challenging and innovative. It should be recognised however that achievement will be difficult in the present national political and economic climate and with current restrictions on budgets. The proposals are put forward as the basis for consultation, and we will continue to consult and learn from the best practice of others as we translate the plans and targets into action." (p. 3)*

Given this lack of firm commitment, it will not be surprising if the action plans remained uncompleted or totally abandoned.

Sadly the public debate that followed the publication of the Bradford Commission report did not include any specific reference to the role the local Pakistani and Bangladeshi communities could play in dealing with some of the serious, subtle and rather controversial issues articulated in the report. Such an omission incorrectly assumed that either these communities were totally incapable, helpless or powerless to do anything about them or, at worst, that they did not matter. I believe that they have an equally, if not more, important role to play because they are central and closer to the issues than anybody else. In relation to the issues raised in the Bradford Commission report, parents and local communities can significantly contribute, for example, in:

♦ checking the development of a youth culture in which drugs, crime prostitution, and religious extremism are becoming acceptable features;

♦ addressing concerns about domestic violence and the lack of freedom for women to pursue their education and careers;

♦ encouraging young people to contribute to the decision-making processes in the family and community, and in making space for them in leadership roles;

♦ encouraging young people to explore employment opportunities in the diverse national labour market;

♦ appreciating the long-term negative consequences of 'transcontinental marriages' ;

- helping to reduce the truancy rate and increase the standards in educational achievements; and
- adding community resources to complement state funded initiatives which address specific issues concerning their particular communities .

The South Asian communities have not fully grasped the implications of a shift in political thinking in relation to government spending on the welfare state. It is likely to pose a serious challenge to the existence of *'dependency culture'* and for those trapped in it. Unless these communities learn to deal with certain issues themselves, social disorders of the kind the city experienced in 1995, are likely to further damage the communities themselves.

The Bradford Commission report on the Manningham riots concluded that understanding between the various minority communities and the wider white communities was seriously deficient. Their clustering reduces interaction and communication between various communities which slows down and impedes the development of a peaceful multicultural community. Equal opportunities initiatives appear to have little real impact on the economic position of these communities. Racial prejudice and discrimination are still strong barriers to the upward social and economic mobility of Asian communities.

Women's peace march after the Mannigham riots
Photograph by the kind permission of T&A, Bradford

9

IT IS NOT THE SAME

The state of race relations in Bradford has changed significantly over the last 50 years. This chapter briefly describes some aspects of these changes and the processes of change.

The popular stereotypes of the past 50 years about British black people as unambitious, irresponsible, lazy, crafty, corrupting and as a dependent under class, with their reactionary subcultures of crime and drugs, have been successfully challenged and have little relevance to any discussions about future race relations in Britain. Such beliefs lead to unnecessary tensions and racial prejudice and tend to present black people as a 'problem' rather than as citizens and a nationally valuable human resource. Likewise, South Asians are seen as ambitious, entrepreneurial and hard working. But also as isolationist, traditionalist and as striving hard to erect social barriers to prevent the erosion of their religious, cultural and linguistic distinctiveness. This assessment of South Asians' position in Britain is also an exaggerated generalisation. Undoubtedly, some sections of South Asians are high achievers in education and are well placed in the labour and housing markets. Their successes sometimes cause greater tensions than their cultural distinctiveness. However, in reality not all of them have overcome their poverty and disadvantage.

Since the early 1980s, 'politically correct' has become everyone's favourite target. Most white people either do not know or find it difficult to use in their spontaneous conversation or comments the so-called 'correct terms' to describe non-white people. They are thus tortured by the prospect of slighting them. Minorities have a different problem with the politically correct: it is one thing to get samosas, saris and steel bands, to visit and organise Punjabi *melas* and West Indian carnivals, it is another to actually do something about racism and inequalities. To black and South Asians this kind of acceptance was the joke of the

1970s. As with many heated issues, many people tried to stay out of the fire, quietly hoping the clamour about multiculturalism would go away so that one day they would be able to go back to their old comfortable ways. However, this has not happened. A multi-cultural society has become the irreversible phenomenon. Multiculturalism in turn has become 'racism awareness'.

In the racism awareness debate, 'power plus prejudice' occupied the central position. Thus political correctness necessitated the challenging of white-male supremacy. The politics of race and power became important ingredients of racism and cultural awareness training courses.

For the first time the management of diversity became an issue in employment practice as well as in the provision of services. The business world began to feel the costly and obstructive effects of trying to manage a diverse workforce without the appropriate training or knowledge of how to do it. This opened up a new field for educated black and South Asian people to become race awareness trainers / advisors. Most of them were without any professional training themselves.

The anti-racism and multiculturalism of the 1980s, with their assumptions about minority ethnic communities as a 'black' unity, have proved to be somewhat flawed. Likewise, the homogeneity of South Asian communities under the blanket term 'Asian' has proved an unworkable concept. The 1990s have witnessed the polarisation of these communities on religious and regional lines.

Culture gives us a fundamental sense of belonging. It helps us to identify with 'we' and differentiate 'us' from 'them'. We all carry cultures the same time, and have layers of eccentric circles of different cultures. Our inherited culture is the core. Our ethnicity, nationality, religion, the generation into which we are born with all its different characteristics, the specific historical times of our growing up, parental and acquired class, sexual orientation - these are the cultural operators which mostly shape our sense of 'we'. In addition to inherited cultures we have acquired cultures: the culture of our professions; immigration orientations, political, social and sect group identities etc. According to Markowitz (1994):

The struggle for racial justice

" The problem the multicultural movement faces is inherent in human civilization; there are few, if any cultures that teach us to be multicultural. We were all raised with the dualistic thinking that human society has traditionally perpetuated-the us/them dichotomy—that makes it so difficult to reach out and embrace differences rather than fearing them or feeling threatened by them. It is hardly surprising that there is no comfortable language of inclusion yet, and that, so far, we stumble along with the stilted patois of the politically correct. "

British multiculturalism has passed the point of no return. It is futile to debate it in terms of immigration statistics or the size of British black and Asian populations. Provocative statements on this subject to score political points serve no valid cause. They only add to the existing fragility of race relations, particularly in the economically less prosperous and socially disadvantaged cities of Britain. The emergence of a black and Asian middle class provides hope for the future, however, it should not be relied upon too much. The problems of the inner city under class are real and therefore, must be addressed in a positive way. The problems of crime, personal security, drugs and disintegrating family life are deeply rooted in the poor and economically disadvantaged inner-city areas. Minority ethnic communities suffer relatively more from these than white residents.

The experience so far shows that economic and political integration is possible; whilst social, cultural and religious integration is probably not possible even if it were desirable. Therefore, economic and civic assimilation is a legitimate and a realistic objective to pursue for race relations and equal opportunity policies. Social, cultural and religious integration is neither possible nor is it desirable. Cultural separatism is dangerous only when it is used to obtain political power. Distinctive socio-religious identities are harmless until exploited by leaderships with vested individual or group interests. For example, South Asian identities are no threat to the British way of life or the interests of whites or to inter-community relations until the leaders of these communities attempt to manipulate the feelings of their members to gain political power. To weaken the possibilities of this happening, the majority community and its local and national institutions must firmly recognise the multi-cultural, multi-faith and multi-racial nature of contemporary British society. In the words of *The Parekh Report (2000)*, "the government should formally declare that the United Kingdom is a multicultural society". They should demonstrate their willingness to accord its minority ethnic communities' equal rights of citizenship and a commitment to share political power and economic rewards.

Sharing the power to shape society is far more than a distant ideal for minorities; it is a survival issue. Ultimately, multiculturalism is a movement to make society a place in which people of all cultures are afforded equal respect, have an equal voice and an equal influence in shaping the values of the larger society. The real issue is that we have to redistribute the meagre pie in the knowledge that resources are finite.

To achieve a fair society without racial inequalities, all local minority ethnic communities and their grassroots leaderships need to be actively involved in the governmental institutions and other voluntary sector organisations. The funding of employment training schemes which simply keep people without jobs off the unemployment register or train them for the type of jobs that do not exist locally, may engender feelings of false security about their effectiveness in dealing with the real issues. Such schemes do not take people out of the dependency culture. Dependency culture is a delayed time bomb for everybody but it is even more dangerous for race relations. It nurtures black frustration, criminal tendencies, the disintegration of family life and consequently, racial tensions.

Changed Expectations and Identities

The life of the ethnic minority communities settled in Bradford has altered beyond recognition. Their general outlook, life-styles and attitudes have changed in some significant ways. Are all these changes a natural part of the process of permanent settlement of minority groups? There is no single simple answer. Some of the changes are a natural outcome of the interaction between 'minority cultures' and the 'indigenous western cultures' whilst others are indicative of completely the opposite, that is the 'reinforcement' of their distinctive traditional cultures and life-styles.

A number of interesting examples can illustrate the point. The point to note is that in many areas a 'give and take' approach is not evident. Take the example of the community languages or mother-tongues of South Asian migrants. In the 1950s through the 1970s, immigrants tried hard (within their limited capacity) to learn English and to use it in the public domain. To speak in their own languages was perceived as an 'offence' to white people. The local white population also expected them to learn English smartly and was reluctant to make allowances for non-English speakers' linguistic limitations. They were intolerant of anyone speaking in Punjabi or any other language. It wasn't uncommon even to see notices in places such as public houses: "No Punjabi Allowed". Interpreters were appointed more to facilitate the communication difficulties of officials dealing with their Asian clients rather than to resolve the problems of immigrants.

This is in complete contrast to the use of community languages in the city in the year 2001. As the main language of communication and medium of education in schools for all children born in the city is English, minority communities emphasise the learning of community languages by their children to preserve their religious and cultural heritage. Even in the presence of English-only understanding people, Asian speakers feel less inhibited to converse in their own language with people of similar background. 'No offence caused', is the normal attitude. Community languages are taught in mainstream educational systems; some street names and notices written in community languages inside and outside many public buildings appear as a norm in Bradford. Many public sector institutions publish literature about their areas of work and services in community languages. Not always with a view to making communication more effective (as the majority of first generation immigrant adults cannot read or write in their own mother-tongues) but to be 'politically correct' in awarding recognition to the languages of the recipients of their services. This change in the use of community languages on 'both sides' of the equation has significant positive as well as negative implications for the kind of multi-ethnic city we aspire towards and what we might actually get in the future.

Alongside the provision of community language teaching in mainstream schools, there is a large collection of books in community languages in the city's libraries. Minority cultural events and arts exhibitions of minority groups' cultural and artistic heritage are fine examples of respect accorded to the diversity of cultures in the city, respect that is a necessary prerequisite for harmonious community relations.

In the 1960s, immigrant workers used to hide their food at work and eat it sitting in remote corners to avoid its smell reaching white noses. On the buses, white passengers would sit seats away to avoid the smell of garlic from the body or clothes of Asian passengers. Now, curries have become the 'national dish', snatching the title from 'fish and chips'. South Asian women who dreaded going out on the streets in their traditional *kameez shalwar* some two decades before, now proudly wear them on all occasions without any fear or inhibition. Men too have become more relaxed about the wearing of western style clothes. Some parts of the inner city look no different from the bazaars of Jalandhar, Mumbai or Lahore. The change is not only symptomatic of the increased confidence of ethnic minority communities and a resurgence of pride in being traditional but is also equally due to the fact that the local white population has changed its expectations.

In Bradford concerns are sometimes expressed publicly but more often quietly and in private circles that the white population and the local institutions have 'given' too much in exchange for almost nothing 'given up' by the minority ethnic communities. There is a strong perception and feeling of almost despondency that the South Asian communities are doing very little in terms of self-help initiatives to deal with their relative economic disadvantage and towards promoting good harmonious community relations in the city.

By the end of 1978, nearly half of the platform staff employed by Bradford Metro was of Asian origin. But, no Asian inspector was appointed until January 1979. The officials of the Transport and General Workers Union, the union representing these employees, believed that no Asian busman then was capable of doing the job of inspector. The District Manager expected a "blacklash from white employees", if an Asian was promoted to the position of inspector. But now, at the turn of the century, South Asians hold even higher senior positions such as the Traffic Manager on the city busses. (1)

Since the appointment of Munawar Hussain as the first alderman in 1972, the political involvement of South Asian communities in local elections is highly significant and such developments are particularly noteworthy. The first Asian Lord Mayor was appointed in 1985 and the second one took office in May 2001. There are currently thirteen councillors of South Asian background, some holding chairmanships of key committees and one who was the Deputy Leader of the Labour Party in control of the Council until May 2000. The city produced its first Asian MP, Marsha Singh in the 1997 general elections.

Social and Religious Celebrations
Annual festive events such as Bradford Mela, and *Eid, Dewali and Vaisakhi* celebrations offer enormous opportunities for inter-community interaction. Bradford Mela, pioneered in Britain some ten years ago, has become an example to follow for all British cities with significant concentrations of South Asian communities. On its own, it has contributed tremendously to the enhancement of the local white population's understanding of South Asian cultures, ways of entertainment and music. The display of lights in the inner city areas and the city centre at *Diwali, Ramadan*, and *Vaisakhi* is an indication of providing some parity to minority religious celebrations with celebrations at Christmas.

In the post-Rushdie incident period some Muslim business and professional people concerned with promoting a positive image of Islam and the Muslim communities of Bradford set up the *Eid Committee*. The Committee has been holding regular religious celebrations to which they invite guests from other communities with a view to developing better understanding between the various ethnic communities of the city.

10

AGENTS OF CHANGE

During the 1960s the prime focus of the activities of all organisations concerned with the 'immigrant problem' remained upon the establishment of good and harmonious 'community relations'. Bradford was hoping to absorb the newcomers as it thought it had done in the case of earlier European immigrant communities. There were rare incidents of protests from the new immigrants themselves about the way they were treated in employment, housing or by the welfare state system in general. Even the blatant discrimination that occurred in public places such as pubs was ignored. If there were any public demonstrations, those were against the immigration legislation that was becoming increasingly unfair and restrictive. Most of the time these protests were joint activities of immigrant organisations such as the Indian Workers' Association together with the national (predominantly white) organisations working in the field of civil liberties.

However, during the 1970s the community relations situation changed significantly. A number of national studies and local incidents clearly and firmly established the presence of racial prejudice, discrimination and racial disadvantage. Most of the immigrant families were re-united and a younger generation of Asian and Afro-Caribbean was becoming visible. The high profile activities of some fascist and racist groups were resulting in increased racial violence and incidents of racial harassment. The response of the younger generation to such anti-immigrant policy and activities became different and more confrontational. By the middle of the1970s the British Campaign to Stop Immigration (the changed name of an earlier Yorkshire-based group formed by Jim Merrick, a local former Conservative councillor) and the National Front had established a strong base in Bradford. They had started fielding candidates in local elections. The development of these racist forces in the city were confronted and counter-balanced by the collaborative actions of groups like the Indian Workers' Association, the International Socialist Workers Party, the International Marxist Group, the Kashmir Welfare Association, the Anti-Nazi League and the Asian Youth Movement. (1)

The struggle for racial justice

The 1980s were largely concerned with the development and implementation of equal opportunity policies dealing with racial discrimination, racial disadvantage and racial attacks. With the increasing number of street disturbances involving young people from minority ethnic backgrounds the social order issues became central in the mid 1990s.

More recently, some serious race riots in Northern cities such as Burnley, Oldham, Leeds and Bradford and the concerns of the authorities about 'self-segregation' and 'polarisation' of minority ethnic communities in these cities, the focus of state policy has shifted towards 'community cohesion' and 'citizenship' programmes.

Changes in the race relations field are the result of the activities of a large number of organisations, individuals and institutions. This chapter provides a brief account of the nature and activities of *some* of the key players who have contributed or are presently contributing to the development of good race relations in Bradford.

There are many other agencies which are omitted here. For instance, a number of business organisations such as Bradford Business Link, Action for Business (Bradford) Limited, Quest for Economic Development, Keighley Asian Business Forum, the Asian Trades Link (Yorkshire), Euro-Asian Resource Centre and Bradford Asian Businesses Association are helping in the development of South Asian businesses in the city and thereby contributing to the economic prosperity of minority ethnic communities. Since the Manningham riots of 1995 and the race riots of 2001, and under the Single Regeneration Budget allocations a number of local youth groups and other organisations have emerged. They are operating schemes to improve race relations in the city and are working towards the elimination of racial inequalities. It is too early to assess or to comment upon their achievements. Bradford & District Training & Enterprise Council (TEC) within its official remit took some modest initiatives in promoting equality of opportunity in employment as described in its 1999-2000 annual report. TEC was closed in March 2001 and is replaced by a bigger regional organisation, the Learning & Skills Council with its headquarters in Bradford.

An assessment of the impact of most voluntary and statutory bodies upon race relations in Bradford was beyond the limited scope of the present book. Likewise, the contributions of NHS bodies in dealing with issues of equality of opportunity in employment and the provision of services are missing here too. The absence of a proper assessment of such contributions from this book is due to limitations of space and readily accessible information and is no reflection on their significance. The roles of Bradford REC and Bradford Metropolitan Council are the subjects of separate chapters.

Role of Churches and Inter-Faith Organisations

Lewis (1992) very well documents the role of churches in the field of community relations and in increasing the acceptance of minorities in the city. For the first five years (1966-1971), Bradford CRC was chaired by the Anglican Bishop of Bradford. Among the officers of the Executive Committee the treasurer was the headmaster of a Roman Catholic Church school and the Reverend Peter Hawkins, an Anglican community relations chaplain who spoke Bengali, also worked very actively in the area of community relations. Again, the Right Reverend Bishop of Bradford, Robert Williamson played a significant role in keeping the dialogue going with the Muslim community during the Rushdie Affair. The good work of churches in race relations is currently (May 2002) being steered by Dr Philip Lewis, community affairs advisor to the Anglican Bishop of Bradford.

A number of other organisations supported by mainstream religious bodies also contributed significantly to the promotion of good community relations in the city. For example, Common Purpose, supported by a charitable trust set up in 1988, offers programmes for people from all sectors and communities interested in the development of a future leadership that would be appropriate for Bradford with its diverse cultural and religious environment. The Inner Cities Religious Council, supported by the government's Action for Cities Programme, has its own activities aimed at improving relations between different

The struggle for racial justice

faith communities in the city. The activities of these organisations have enhanced cross-community involvement in the celebration of religious festivals. The contributions of some of these organisations are briefly described below.

The Century to Millennium Project (C2M): C2M was established with a substantial grant of half a million pounds from the Millennium Commission in 1998. It is working with local communities and awards grants to local projects. Its first round of awards had a particular emphasis on Bradford's 'Areas of Stress'. Its list of second round awards includes some small projects directly concerned with issues relating to Asian women and racism in sport. The activities of the C2M are aimed at 'community development' and the empowerment of poor communities. Its partners as grant holders sponsor activities that are likely to have positive impacts on race relations in the city.

Touchstone Centre: The Touchstone Centre in Bradford was established about 10 years ago by the Methodist Church. "Touchstone is a movement of faith expressing the good news of Christ through the word, deeds and lives of those who share a vision for the city". Touchstone's main activities are focused on the Christian communities in inner city areas but, because of its location and spatial areas of operation, it is becoming increasingly in touch with minority ethnic communities and the particular social and religious issues that concern them. For example, Molly Kenyon, a worker at the centre produced a report on the Manningham Riots, which was commissioned by Touchstone. (2)

Life Force: Life Force was a new leisure attraction opened in 2000 in St. Peter's House in central Bradford. It was designed to explore faith and belief from all ages and cultures through dynamic interactive experiences. It claimed to be unique to the UK and planned to celebrate the main religious festivals of the various faiths in the city. Although it was expected to be a major tourist attraction in Bradford, it failed to achieve the visitor numbers it needed. Its closure less than a year after its inception meant that its genuine potential for fostering understanding between diverse local communities was sadly never realised.

Curry Project: The Curry Project is a good example of a working partnership between various faith communities in Bradford in providing meals for homeless people in the city. The project was started by Lachhman Singh, a Sikh who felt that the large amounts of cooked food left over in Sikh temples after the Sunday langar should be distributed to homeless people. Over the years, the project has grown in size, has attracted more volunteers across other faiths, and is firmly rooted through occasional grants from Bradford Council.

Inter-Faith Education Centre (IEC): Mohammed Ajeeb, Bradford's first Asian Lord Mayor, opened IEC in 1986. The Centre employs more than a dozen staff from various faith communities. They provide advice and support to local teachers with the multi-faith curriculum of religious education. They facilitate schools' liaison with local community groups and religious places of worship. Tutors from the Centre sometimes lead separate faith group meetings in schools. It is also a major resource centre for materials on the various faiths represented in the city. Other than teachers, people from professions such as nurses, police officers, social workers and employees of other local companies have also used IEC's staff and material resources to develop and enhance their knowledge of the minority ethnic communities in the city. Since its inception the Centre has fulfilled a vital role in developing harmonious relations between different faith communities in Bradford through raising local professional people's understanding and awareness of the culturally and religiously diverse population of the city. Bradford Concord Faith Society meets regularly at the IEC and holds talks on inter-faith topics and arranges discussions on a wide range of social and religious issues involving minority ethnic communities.

Q21: Centre for Dialogue and Action: This project, which was initiated by the Inter-Faith Education Centre in 1995, was located in the same building as the Centre but was separately managed by a Board of Trustees. The Q21 charitable company had the support of 130 individuals and 20 organizational members over its 6 years existence. It aimed to deal with questions facing Bradford in the 21st century. It followed an ambitious programme of activities relating to a wide range of issues of mutual concern to all communities in Bradford in order to foster a culture of peaceful co-existence in the city. It aimed to achieve its goals through education, partnership and collaboration. The project had great long-term potential to contribute towards improving race relations in Bradford. Sadly, largely through lack of funding and human resources it had to close down in May 2002.

SIGNING . . . Coun Mohammed Ajeeb and the Rt Rev David Smith, front, with other city leaders

Leaders back racism fight

RELIGIOUS and political leaders in Bradford showed a united front to launch the fight against racism.

Leading members of the community came together at City Hall for the signing of the pioneering Bradford Charter, which declares the city a no-go area for fascists.

The charter follows the recent British National Party election victory in Tower Hamlets and is the idea of the new anti-fascist organisation, the United Front against Racism and Fascism.

Guests at the launch included the Lord Mayor of Bradford, Councillor Bob Sowman; the Bishop of Bradford, the Right Reverend David Smith; leaders of both the city's Labour and Conservative parties, and Muslim, Hindu and Sikh leaders.

On Tuesday, members of the council will be asked to support the charter and make it a part of Bradford Council policy.

Councillor Mohammed Ajeeb, who spearheaded the new organisation, said: "We want to keep our community

clear of these people who create trouble."

Councillor Ronnie Farley, leader of the council's Conservative group, said: "We want to show that ordinary people in Bradford do not accept bigotry in our community."

● Extra police officers were today drafted into the east end of London amid fears of violence at a huge anti-racist march. Around 20,000 people were expected to join the march organised by the Anti-Nazi League.

Telegraph & Argus 16 October 1993

African-Caribbean Organisations (3)

There is very little known about the work of the African Caribbean organisations in Bradford and in fact even general information about the black communities in the city is difficult to obtain. It is widely recognised that black communities in Bradford have been ignored in any serious discussions in the formulation of policies concerning race, cultural diversity and economic inequalities. The overall size of these communities is about 6,300 (1998) and they constitute 1.3% of the total population and 6.2 % of the total ethnic minority population in Bradford. Being a minority within the ethnic minority population and because of their wide spatial dispersion they do not often make 'media headlines'. However, in reality they suffer in the same way from racial harassment and social and economic inequalities, as do South Asian ethnic groups in the city. Prior to the end of the 1970s the **Credit Union** and the **Dominican Association**, lead by Murray Celaire, were two small bodies known to have provided contacts between white and West Indian communities in the city. The role of some black organisations in serving the needs of their communities and their contribution to race relations are briefly described below.

In 1978 **the West Indian Community Centre Association** was established. The Association obtained a licence to open a club at Textile Hall in Westgate in order to provide the community with a place to meet, sing and dance. In 1981 the club was destroyed by fire and was then re-opened as **Checkpoint** in August 1983 after refurbishing costs of £100, 000, including a grant of £70, 000 from Bradford Council. Checkpoint remained the focal point of social activities of the city's black population. People such as Courtney Hay and Erskine Grant, associated with the running of the centre, continuously attempted to keep the issues concerning the local black community on the policy makers' agenda. During the mid-1980s a row developed between Bradford Council and the centre management about its non-submission of accounts regarding the grant from the Council. The centre was also alleged to be more involved in political activities than in its function as a community centre.

Another organisation, the **West Indian Parents' Association** was set up in 1978.This was largely concerned with the educational issues relating to black children in local schools. Joseph Flerin chaired the WIPA for a number of years. It started running Saturday classes for black children to improve their achievement standards in schools and to offer them classes in Caribbean history and cultures. Initially based in Manningham it later moved to Mannvile Terrace near Bradford College. Due to the lack of financial support from public sector organisations WIPA's activities gradually folded.

More recently, the **African-Caribbean Economic Establishment (ACEE)** founded in 1994 as a result of the study carried out in Bradford to explore the particular problems of African-Caribbean people in employment, education, business and training, has become the leading organisation of the local black population under the leadership of Karl Oxford. The Joseph Rowntree Charitable Trust and Bradford Council funded the study. It is an example of good practice in an area that was

63

only given a marginal concern in race relations discussions and policy development in the city in the past. The **Afro-Caribbean Resource Centre**, established in August 1999, is also very active in promoting the cultural and social aspects of the black population and is getting actively involved in regeneration and community development initiatives.

South Asian Religious Organisations

There are more than a hundred mosques, temples and gurdwaras in the city. Their prime function is to provide facilities for routine religious worship, celebration of religious and social functions, and facilities for the teaching of community languages of their respective faith groups. Because of their unique position in encompassing almost the entire Hindu, Muslim and Sikh populations of the city they have served as the main point of contact between white and non-white communities, and private and public sector institutions. The focus of their activities has been typically on conservation and the valuing of their respective religious and cultural heritages. There is little evidence in their activities of account being taken of the present context in which their followers are conducting their lives and creating new cultures: hybrids of traditional South Asian value systems and norms of life mixed with western life styles.

Race relations have never been their central concern. Most of the time they have only reacted to those incidents or developments which were thwarting their efforts in the processes of preserving and promoting their traditional religious and cultural practices. There is always a place for the conservation and celebration of traditions which serve to maintain distinctive identities but not by ignoring the realities of the wider world around. Most of these organisations have not proactively embraced many of the specific programmes and activities designed to foster better understanding between their own and the white communities in the city. Nevertheless, they generally responded very positively to the initiatives taken by the representatives of white communities in making the social, cultural and civic environment of Bradford all-inclusive. For instance, minority ethnic communities had full representation in the enthronement ceremony of Bishop of Bradford (1984), the memorial service for those who died in the Bradford City football ground fire (1985), the welcome for Archbishop Desmond Tutu (1988) and the visits of Her Majesty the Queen and other members of the royal family in the 1990s. This level of civic integration may look more symbolic than substantive, but at least it demonstrates the minority communities', as well as the white institutions', willingness and desire for close co-operation in making the city a "community of communities".

The scope of this study does not allow for an in depth examination of the work of these organisations individually. In order to capture the overall perspective of these religious organisation on race issues the role and activities of the umbrella organisations of the three religious communities, Muslim, Hindu and Sikh, are discussed here in order to indicate the role they play or have played in shaping the race relations environment in Bradford.

Bradford Council for Mosques: The early part of the 1980s saw the emergence of umbrella organisations for different faith communities in Bradford. The first to come on the scene was the Bradford Council for Mosques in 1981. Prior to this there has been no major organisation to present a broadly acceptable Muslim perspective on a wide range of issues, arising mainly in the field of education. With the increasing number of mosques in the city it was becoming difficult for the local authority and other public sector bodies to consult the Muslim community on whatever limited policy proposals they had on minority ethnic communities' issues. Thus the setting up of the Council for Mosques was a welcome initiative, encouraged and supported by the local authority. The Council received funds from the local authority for setting up its premises, perhaps the first among all ethnic minority organisations to receive such support. Whatever the status of the Council within the local Muslim population, as explained in other appropriate sections of the book, it has made a significant overall positive impact upon the shaping of race relations in the city over the last two decades. As explained elsewhere in the book its role in the *Rushdie Affair*, the *Halal* meat debate and the *Honeyford Affair* earned it a unique status in Bradford and outside, a status that it still enjoys.

Federation of Bradford Sikh Organizations: During the period of development of multicultural policies in the 1980s, the Bradford

Council of Mosques received a fair amount of high profile attention in the local media. Sikh and Hindu communities became increasingly concerned that their views on local issues were likely to be marginalised or ignored unless they raised their collective voices as well. Hitherto, only some Hindu and Sikh influential individuals represented their communities' views and concerns. Thus the need to establish similar parallel umbrella organisations became an urgent one. The Federation of Bradford Sikh Organisations came into being in 1984, ironically not as a result of the above concern but in response to the events in the Punjab that were reflecting badly on the media image of Sikhs in Britain. Right from the beginning the Federation remained occupied in developing unity and cohesiveness within the Sikh community and its organisations in order to counter the influences of external events. This preoccupation of the Federation with matters largely internal to the local Sikh community limited its ability to contribute to inter-community relations.

Vishwa Hindu Parishad (UK): Vishwa Hindu Parishad (UK) set up its Yorkshire branch, based in Bradford, in 1984. Although a national organisation, it tried to represent the views of Bradford Hindus. VHP's strong links with the Indian right-wing Hindu organisation, Rashtria Swayamsevak Sangh, has always put a question mark on its status as the representative organization of local Hindus. On the whole, its contribution to race relations is no greater than other local Hindu organisations such as the Hindu Cultural Society or the Bharitya Mandal.

Joint Committee of Asian Organisations (JCAO): At Bradford CRC's 1987 annual election, most of the senior official positions were taken by young people. The majority of them were Bradford Council employees working in race-related jobs. This raised serious concerns within the three faith umbrella organisations about the future direction of the CRC. The Hindu Cultural Society's representatives on the CRC had been expressing their concern about the CRC's bias in favour of Muslim organisations and threatened to dissociate from it. The Federation of Bradford Sikh Organisations had already raised a number of issues about its membership and activities with the Senior CRO. There was a potential threat of it withdrawing its support if those issues were not addressed quickly. The Council for Mosques had already withdrawn its membership.

However, the important fact was that up till then the CRC had been the only forum at which any inter-faith community issues or mutual concerns about local policies could be discussed. Their weakening confidence in the CRC led them to set up the Joint Committee of Asian Organisations (JCAO). JCAO did not adopt a formal statement of its objectives and it remained a semi-formal forum of some key individuals from the three faith umbrella organisations. It continued to meet regularly to discuss issues of mutual interest and concern for almost four years. However, it gradually lost momentum and became dysfunctional.

Inter-Faith Group: Fortunately, the gap was filled with the emergence of the Inter-Faith Group, established at the initiative of the Bishop of Bradford in the early 1990s. The ad hoc, informal initiatives of the Bishop to mediate during the Rushdie Affair and the Gulf War Crisis continued on a more formal basis in the shape of the Inter-Faith Group. This group has been meeting fairly regularly since 1992 under the chairmanship of the Right Reverend David J Smith. The Group has maintained a membership of committed individual from the Hindu, Sikh and Muslim communities and holds its meetings at different religious centres in turn. Over the years it has discussed a wide range of topics in education, health, inter-community tensions, race relations, representation of faith communities in local regeneration initiatives and so on. The presence and the work of the Group are very positive elements in keeping the lines of communication open at all times between the various faith communities, communities that otherwise have only fairly limited interaction.

Non-Religious Organisations

Asian Youth Movement: The earliest significant activities of the Asian Youth Movement (AYM established in 1978)) were in the middle of the 1980s. It organised protests against racial attacks and harassment in Bradford schools, marches and protests against the National Front and British National Party activities and demonstrations against the allegedly racist immigration legislation. On a couple of occasions it also formed defence committees to fight against specific deportation cases. To start with AYM drew its members from all the Asian communities, however this across-communities composition did not survive for too long. With the development of a high profile equal opportunity approach by the local authority in the 1980s, some members of the AYM got jobs with the authority as racism awareness trainers and policy development officers which led to the gradual disintegration of the movement.

The Indian Workers' Association, Great Britain: IWA (GB) is perhaps one of the oldest Indian organisations in Britain. It was established in 1938 in Coventry by a handful of Indian workers. It remained dormant for a long period. It was re-launched in 1953 and by 1957 had branches in most cities of Indian settlement. It aimed at organising Indian immigrants for participation in political activities. The national and local leadership of the IWA consisted of two major groups: moderate entrepreneurs and political radicals. The two factions of the IWA reflected the factions within the Communist Party of India. For most of the time, they worked as rivals in Britain and likewise in Bradford. In principle the IWA is a non-religious organisation, however, the local IWAs maintained close contact with local gurdwaras (Sikh temples).

In the early sixties the IWA organised campaigns and demonstrations against the National Front and other right-wing organisations. The IWA's anti-racism and anti-discrimination activities attracted a good deal of general support from Bradford Indians. However their pre-occupation with Indian politics alienated them from their grassroots membership.

IWA (M-L) won credibility in the late 1970s by playing an effective leading role in two local issues concerning the South Asian community. It mobilised strong parental opposition to the racially discriminatory 'bussing policy' of the local Educational Services Committee. The policy was investigated by the Commission for Racial Equality and eventually scrapped. It also launched a strong protest against racial discrimination in the recruitment and promotion practices of the West

The story of Bradford 1950-2002

Yorkshire Passenger Transport Executive, the allegation that resulted in a successful formal investigation by the Commission for Racial Equality. Both IWAs in Bradford are, at present, small groups of activists. Their present activities are extremely limited, one is running a day centre on Leeds Road for older people whilst the other has shifted its focus from political to purely social activities and individual advice.

Quest for Economic Development Limited (QED): QED was established in 1990 as a company limited by guarantee and is a registered charity. Mohammed Ali and Adeeba Malik, two young, able and committed successful professionals lead it. It now operates well beyond its original Bradford boundaries. It describes its work as: " QED helps to support minority ethnic communities to participate freely and fully in economic, social and public life in the UK. In particular QED offers programmes which broaden and strengthen opportunities in employment, education, business enterprise and the community." Its annual review for 1998-99 claims that it works with 400 individuals and 150 organisations in the four key economic development areas: education, employment, enterprise and community development. It lists well over 50 organisations that support the work of QED through financial or in-kind contributions. The range of its activities stretches from running practical projects to providing training, consultancy services and holding seminars, conferences and community consultation exercises. Its chairman, Tim Ratcliffe says, "QED's work is starting to bridge the gap in understanding between minority and majority communities and mainstream businesses and institutions."

Bradford Alliance Against Racial Harassment (BAAH): The Crime and Disorder Audit (1998) of the City of Bradford Metropolitan District established that the number of reported racially motivated incidents had increased over the previous three years. Almost two thirds of the reported cases were in the category of violence and racial abuse and another 20 per cent were racial harassment and racially motivated damage. To tackle the problem of racially motivated crime, Bradford has adopted a multi-agency partnership approach.

BAARH was set up as a partnership of key agencies to deal with cases of racial harassment. Pilot projects were introduced first in 1996/97 in Canterbury and Little Horton and later extended to Bradford 3. It was a

69

partnership between West Yorkshire Police, Bradford Council, Bradford Racial Equality Council and some other voluntary organisations. It started with a small European Union grant but attracted a large sum of £319K from the National Lotteries Charities Board in 1998. Before the alliance could make a real contribution to support the victims of racial harassment and racial attacks it got into trouble, its Project Officer sacked for alleged misappropriation of funds and BREC blamed for its bad overall management. Sadly, an urgently needed and extremely important organisation with good potential for dealing with highly sensitive issues in race relations found itself in disrepute by the end of 1999.

The Bradford and District Minority Ethnic Communities' Police Liaison Committee: Relations between the police and particularly the Muslim community in the city had in reality been fairly tense and fragile right through the 1990s despite public claims by the police that they had been "good". This liaison committee is the latest police initiative to enhance co-operation between the police and minority ethnic communities. The Home Office Minister Paul Boateng launched the Committee on 18 June 1999. The press release described it as an "exciting new partnership in race relations in Bradford" and "a key to the future of harmonious race relations" in the district. The Committee intends to build trust and confidence between the police and minority ethnic communities. It is hoped that the Committee will bring people together to discuss and resolve issues and problems which affect their communities. Currently, the Committee has 30 people drawn from a wide range of backgrounds across the communities, businessmen, magistrates, media personalities, accountants, community leaders and so on. The Committee has been awarded over £273K of government funding for its activities. It is too early (November 2001) to assess the effectiveness of this high profile initiative.

Role of the Local Press, Minority Arts and the Media

The press and the media in Britain have generally been accused of having a reactionary and fairly negative approach to race-related issues. The T&A, the local newspaper has contributed to community and race relations in the city in its own way. Occasionally, it was criticised for its negative and reactionary approach to local race relations issues. However, for the last few years the T&A's approach to race relations has been objective, balanced and positive looking. For example, it won the media award from the Commission for Racial Equality for its fair, comprehensive, balanced and sensitive reporting of the Manningham Riots of 1995. Its initiatives such as an Urdu column for its non-English speaking readers in the 1970s provided recognition and an increased respect towards minority cultures. Saturday's T&A carries a feature "Faith Matters" that covers news and information about events and celebrations of all religions including minority faiths. It also publishes every month the Asian Eye, a special supplement in English for the South Asian communities. All these initiatives may have a strong commercial objective but their positive impact on inter-community relations cannot be ignored. The T & A's coverage of the riots of July 2001 and the Lord Ouseley Report have been just superb. Its policy to provide coverage to all types of community initiatives and projects, big or small, aimed at improving inter-community relations, is impressive and highly appreciated by minority ethnic community groups.

Oriental Arts, a 14 year-old group that promotes artists from India, *bhangra* groups and musical concerts has contributed to the development of Bradford as a city of diverse cultures. It has worked with South Asian, Chinese, Japanese and Ukrainian communities in hosting their entertainment events. It was sponsored and supported by Bradford Council for a number of years. Asian arts group Kala Sangam is also promoting Asian cultures in the city.

Bradford has its own Asian radio station, Bradford City Radio (called Sunrise Radio since 1991) started in 1989. Different faith communities acquire short-term licences to relay programmes to celebrate their specific religious festivals such as *Ramadan, Diwali, Vaisakhi* etc. On the one hand, such activities profoundly enrich the social and cultural environment for all Bradfordians to enjoy. On the other hand, they promote the distinctive cultural and religious identities of minority communities that could be perceived as divisive and therefore an obstacle in the path of developing cohesive future community relations.

Bradford Congress / Bradford Vision (4)

Working towards achieving racial justice is not the responsibility and preserve of only some voluntary sector organisations, it is a major expectation of all institutions. In the area of race equality work, Bradford Congress has been trying to co-ordinate and to monitor the initiatives of some of its key member organisations in the city. After the publication of its report on the Manningham riots of 1995, Bradford Congress asked its members to give their individual responses to the report. Bradford Chamber of Commerce, Bradford & District Training & Enterprise Council, Bradford Health Authority, Bradford University, Bradford & Ilkley Community College, West Yorkshire Police and Bradford Metropolitan District Council reported the steps they were taking in their respective areas of work and responsibility. As expected, the responses were so varied and service specific, that even to attempt to present a meaningful analysis of them would be beyond the scope of this book.

After the publication of the Macpherson Report on the Stephen Lawrence Inquiry in 1998, Bradford Congress invited its member organisations once again to consider the implications of the recommendations made in the report in the specific context of their individual areas of operation. The Congress received the responses from the organisations mentioned in the above paragraph. Most of the responses referred to their earlier reports on Bradford Commission reports, highlighting progress made on the action plans or initiatives contained in those reports. Sadly, most of the responses read like bureaucratic paper exercises, routine work they should be doing anyway, nothing novel, unique or exciting being proposed that might have the potential to demonstrate significant progress in the near future. Following the publication of the Ouseley Report and the Home Office Reports in response to the race riot in the city in July 2001 the reconstituted Bradford Congress, the Bradford Vision is given a similar responsibility for co-ordinating the action plans of its partners for the implementation of recommendations made in these reports.

11

BRADFORD RACIAL EQUALITY COUNCIL

A Chequered History

On 17 January 1966 Henry Patton, Town Clerk of Bradford, arranged a meeting in the City Hall to discuss the formation of the Bradford Consultative Council for Commonwealth Immigrants (BCCCI). The Right Reverend Michael Parker, the Lord Bishop of Bradford, chaired the meeting. The meeting set up a steering committee to prepare a constitution for the BCCCI. A further meeting on 28 February 1966 which was attended by the local MPs, the Chief Constable, leaders of the local political parties, chairs of key statutory services and their heads, some representatives of local churches and immigrant organisations adopted the constitution proposed by the steering committee. The following were agreed as the objectives of the BCCCI:

(a) The Council shall seek to create understanding between Commonwealth citizens and other citizens of Bradford and shall encourage and promote such actions as may lead to the creation of real a community.

(b) The Council shall seek the goodwill of the City Council to which body it shall from time to time report its deliberations, if requested.

(c) The Council in caring for the general well-being of Commonwealth citizens shall co-operate with statutory authorities and voluntary organisations.

In addition to those present at the meeting it was agreed to extend an invitation to another 25, mainly immigrant organisations to join BCCCI. The full BCCCI formally met for the first time on 17 May 1966 and elected its first honorary officers.

The local authority agreed to finance secretarial support and to provide accommodation for the BCCCI. John E Naylor, a retired police officer, was appointed the first Liaison Officer from 1 February 1966. With his appointment BCCCI became fully operational from its small office in 1a, Upper Piccadilly.

The principal aim of the BCCCI was to facilitate the processes of dealing with problems emerging from the presence of black and Asian new arrivals in the city rather than having an independent proactive stance on fighting the racial prejudice and discrimination that new Commonwealth citizens were facing. This aim was consistent with the approach of the nationally established Community Relations Commission with the main objective being to promote harmonious relations between the various racial groups.

The BCCCI's lack of commitment to fighting racist political attitudes was exposed when its chairman refused to take a resolution condemning Enoch Powell's notorious *"rivers of blood"* speech at its annual general meeting on 28 April 1968. Representatives of the CARE, the Afro-West Indian Society and the United Sikh Association resigned in protest.

Name Change

The BCCCI changed its name to Bradford Community Relations Council (CRC) on 14 April 1969 under guidance from the national Community Relations Commission to all such bodies concerned with community relation in the country. In June 1972 CRC moved to 1 Marlborough Road, Manningham Lane. With the 1974 reorganisation of local authorities, Bradford CRC became Bradford Metropolitan District Community Relations Council on 1 April 1974. Despite the formal name change it remained popularly known as Bradford CRC. However, its activities were extended to cover new areas beyond the old Bradford boundaries to include places like Keighley which had a significant presence of Pakistani and Bangladeshi families.

1970s: Years of Education and Promotion

Up to the mid-1970s, the major role of the Bradford CRC was largely determined by the activities of the Senior CRO, John Naylor and the individual interests of the other two CROs. John Naylor spent most of his time on the activities that suited his own interests, personality, and commitment. Such activities included:

♦ Dealing with the human and personal problems of individuals who approached or were referred to him by others.

♦ Assisting immigrant organisations in holding music concerts, sports festivals and cultural /social functions.

♦ Liasing with the police in disputes between neighbours, giving advice in illegal immigrant cases, making passport enquiries, contacting passport offices and immigration authorities regarding the issuing of Entry Certificates, entry refusal applications and appeals.

♦ Organising visits from high commissions, foreign dignitaries, government officials and ministers and at a lower level for researchers, journalists and students.

♦ In 1972-73 a good deal of work was done to deal with the arrival of immigrants from Uganda despite the fact that only a handful of these families arrived in Bradford

Policy Review 1977

After the passing of the Race Relations Act 1976 Bradford CRC carried out its first major policy review at a policy planning conference held on 15th January 1977. Professor Sheila Allen of Bradford University and Mr. A Haynes from the Community Relations Commission addressed the conference. The conference debated at some length the CRC's aims and objectives, and the policy and practice needed to achieve them. It agreed the following:

A. The aims and objectives of the CRC will be to:
• Eliminate racial discrimination in a multi-cultural society.
• Achieve racial equality by fighting against racialism.
• Promote equality of opportunity between people of different races and cultures.
B. The policy of the CRC will be to:
• Mobilise public opinion by educational and other campaigns, and to protest against racial discrimination in any sphere of life.
• Monitor the policies of the Local Authority and its various departments, employers, trade unions, and other institutions, with a view to influencing them when necessary.

- Help individual members of minority groups who need personal help, if this help cannot be obtained from existing statutory and voluntary agencies.
- Lay particular emphasis on youth work.
- Fight against discrimination affecting not only black minority groups, but also other minorities whenever discrimination was made on the basis of race.

C. For policy implementation the CRC will:

♦ Ask Bradford Metropolitan Council to join the CRC in setting up machinery, to include both elected members and officers of the Local Authority as appropriate, to ensure that the views of minority groups are heard in all matters which affect them. Through such machinery the CRC would expect to be consulted about public policies in relevant fields.

♦ Extend the existing panels or create appropriate sub-committees dealing with various subjects, and involve in those panels or sub-committees people who have responsibilities in the fields of education, health, employment, housing etc.

♦ Press for proper and effective representation of minority groups on all public bodies.

♦ Assist the development of organisations within the minority ethnic groups, and support such organisations without interfering with their leadership on internal policies.

♦ Apply to the Commission for a considerable planned expansion of full-time staff to implement these policies; to maintain pressure on the local authority to increase its financial support; and to utilise schemes such as Urban Aid, Section 11, Job Creation and others to obtain additional staff.

♦ Review membership of the Council and make this subject to annual reconsideration in order to cut out organisations no longer offering effective support.

♦ Review the place of individually invited Council members with a view to reducing their number (these two suggestions would involve alterations to the Constitution).

♦ The Executive Committee to consider setting up sub-committees for week-by-week monitoring of situations, for example, a Finance and Management Subcommittee.

- ◆ Consider setting up a junior executive.
- ◆ Continue individual casework but not to allow this to take precedence over other functions of the Council.

The changes adopted in the aims and objectives as well as in the operational strategy were radical. They required a major shift in the CRC's role as an organisation hitherto primarily concerned with improving "community relations" to working towards "elimination of racial discrimination and disadvantage". Such a change was consistent with the changes in the race relations legislation brought about by the Race Relations Act 1976 by which the Community Relations Commission was replaced by the Commission for Racial Equality (CRE).

Winds of Change
Following the policy review a number of changes took place in the composition of the CRC Council, staffing and the direction of activities.

In its early years the CRC was supported and managed by representatives of religious organisations. Leaders of the local churches were actively involved and played a significant part in the activities of the CRC. For instance, the Right Reverend Michael Parker, the Lord Bishop of Bradford served as the first chairman of the BCCCI for the period 1966-71. For years the representatives of various churches and white religious organisations dominated the membership of the CRC's Executive Committee. Most of the black and Asian members of the CRC were either the representatives of ethnic minority organisations or had very close connections with their respective religious places of worship.

Bradford CRC was criticised from two very different positions. Gurnam Singh Sanghera, a leader of the local branch of the Indian Workers' Association [IWA (GB)] was always critical of the activities of the "semi-sponsored" official community relations organisations, national and local, for being tools in the hands of governments to gloss over the presence of white racism in Britain as an integral part of capitalistic strategy of exploitation of the working classes. It was a reflection of his and the Association's leftist, Marxist political ideology. Partly, his anti-CRC position was due to the personal rivalry between him and the leaders of the local Indian Association who had a much closer working relationship with the CRC officers. Despite his commitment to fight racial discrimination, Sanghera aspired to remain the sole recognised leader of the Indians in the city.

Abdullha Patel and Riaz Shahid, two other staunch critics of the CRC, came from the Muslim Parents' Association. They professed that the dominant Christian hegemony was being used subtly in all policy developments about immigration and immigrant issues and overtly in schools to destroy the Muslim way of life. Both groups wanted to shoot from outside and were not prepared to work for changes from within. On the whole, they remained at the margins and were largely ignored.

Bradford Muslim Parents' Association and particularly its leader Abdullha Patel, who was also a member of the Coloured Peoples' Union, was an ardent critic and opponent of the CRC. He believed that the CRC's set up was "a farce" and that it lacked adequate representation of immigrant organisations (T&A,15 April 1969). Again, he objected to the co-option of a CRC representative on the Immigrant Education Working Party of the Local Education Authority (LEA) who happened to be a Sikh. (T&A, 5 March 1975)

In the year 1977-78 the composition of the CRC membership included 77 organisations and 22 individuals. Almost half of the member organisations were South Asian and the rest of them were largely other religious / voluntary groups. From the very beginning of the BCCCI the role of the religious organisations in the work of the BCCI and the CRC remained significant. Because of his personal religious commitment and his wider contacts with the religious organisations of all denominations in Bradford, John Naylor was able to involve a number of prominent religious leaders of Jewish, Sikh, Muslim, Hindu and Christian churches.

In the year 1977 two new white CROs, Tim Whitfield, Youth CRO and Stephen Ashworth, Employment CRO joined the existing team of John Naylor, Senior CRO and Mr. S S Badan, Education CRO.

Mohammed Ajeeb was elected the first black/Asian chairman of the CRC in 1967-77. The out-going chairman Tom Crehan, who lost the election by only one vote saw Ajeeb's election as chairman as "a dangerous change". He expressed his concern that a black leader might result in the alienation of white membership of the CRC Council. Of his defeat he said: "I am slightly disturbed by it because it seems to represent a trend which is perhaps towards confrontation and a sharpening of issues between immigrants and the host population." (T&A, 27 April 1976)

For the first and only time a member of the CRC Council was expelled when Bernard Slater, a Bradford Grammar School teacher, was expelled for blaming immigrants for smuggling drugs and evading taxes on BBC 2's Open Door documentary on the British Campaign to Stop Immigration (BCSI). (T& A, 24 April 1976) Slater argued that the CRC should represent the views of society at large and not become an immigrant pressure group. Furthermore, he would support an application for membership of the CRC by Jim Merrick, a leading member of the BCSI and a leading spirit of the National Front in Bradford. Such views coming from a long-term member of the CRC caused offence to, and outrage among, all members of the Council.

In 1978, Mohammed Ajeeb's statement that "the total absence of any black face in Parliament indicates the sheer hypocrisy, sophistry and chicanery of political parties", stirred serious controversy. The statement attracted strong condemnation as being 'racist'. A local councillor demanded his resignation from the CRC. (T&A, 8 November 1978)

Towards the end of the 1970s, black and South Asian youths were organising themselves and becoming politically active. For example, a strong local Asian Youth Movement (AYM) emerged in the wake of a significant increase in the activities of the National Front in the city. In 1977 National Front members smashed the windows of the CRC office at Marlborough Road ten times. The AYM started protesting against the activities of extreme rightwing organisations such as the National Front, the British National Party and the Stop Immigration Campaign.

With the appointment of Tim Whitfield as its youth officer, the CRC forged and firmed up its links with the Bradford West Indian

Community Centre Association, Rashtriya Swayamsewak Sangh, the Young Bengali Radicals and the AYM.

In the year 1978-79 CRC brought a number of cases of racial discrimination in public houses: the Royal in Thorn Street, the Merry Mason in Kings Road, the Royal Standard in Manningham Lane, and the Bentley Arms in Bradford 7. It also dealt with cases of discrimination at the Bradford Moor Post Office and the police mistreatment of two Indians. In 1979-80, the CRC dealt with 185 cases in employment including 86 cases of unfair dismissal, 26 cases of discrimination and provided advice and support in 73 cases of redundancy.

In line with its new policy the CRC held a number of meetings with the local authority on its proposal to establish Consultative Links Panels for all its directorates.

1980s: High Profile Years of Change

Interest in the work of the CRC was so strong in the 1980s that in 1980-81 membership of the Council shot up to 120 including 90 representatives from organisations and 30 individual members. It was at this time that a younger group of South Asian members aspired to take over the leadership of the CRC. In May 1987 Ishtiaq Ahmed became chairman of the CRC. Mohammed Salam and Raj Parmar became vice chairs. They were described as "Young Turks" in some circles.

The organisation also had a change in staffing. John Naylor retired in December 1980 and Tim Whitfield succeeded him as Senior CRO in February 1981. Following his appointment, the roles of the officers were reviewed and the CRC moved into new premises at 2 Spring Bank Place. Swaran Singh Badan who had served the CRC since October 1972 also retired on medical ground in August 1987.

In Bradford (and elsewhere too) a debate had started that the CRC had outlived its usefulness for a number of reasons. Firstly, it was argued that the black and Asian communities no longer needed a mediator to express their concerns. Furthermore, some new advice centres in the voluntary sector had emerged in the city to assist these communities in dealing with casework. Secondly, the CRC's major involvement was with the local authority. And the local authority had developed its own internal race-relations machine, that is, it had its own race trainers, community consultative panels, policy development officers and a number of equal opportunity working parties. Finally, awareness of the development of equal opportunity policies had increased in the private sector thus reducing the need for support from a small organisation such as the CRC.

Those who supported the continuation of the CRC nevertheless argued that it was neither a black organisation nor was it there to represent black organisations. It was supporting black and Asian organisations and campaigns for good relations and equal opportunities as an independent organisation in its own right. Secondly, its activities might have been so far limited only to the local authority but it had a much wider potential remit. Compared with any newly created structures within the Local Authority and other major organisations the CRC had a much lengthier experience and expertise in the field of race-relations. However, the CRC accepted that its traditional manner of operation was due for critical review and particularly it had to stop doing casework which duplicated the responsibilities of other voluntary and public sector organisations and agencies. (CRC's Annual report, 1978-88)

The 1980s became the period of the CRC's most intensive work with Bradford Council. Equal opportunities became a major political slogan of the 1980s. The early 1980s saw a strong working relationship developing between the CRC and Bradford Council. In 1981-82 a lot of time was spent developing the Council's Race Relation Policy. The CRC was represented on the newly established Race Relations Advisory Group (RRAG) to oversee the implementation of this policy. This not only enhanced the status and role of the CRC but also stretched its resources to the limit through demands on its staff to be consulted on almost the entire workings of the Council. To widen its field of consultation RRAG decided to have regular meetings with individual ethnic minority organisations in the city. The role of the CRC in reshaping the practices of the Council in many service areas, particularly in employment, was to provide advice, to organise pressure upon particular issues and to assist in maintaining contact with minority ethnic communities. Mohammed Ajeeb took over RRAG's chairmanship and advocated the direct representation of ethnic minority groups, but that was never achieved. RRAG continued to function up to the mid-1980s but gradually lost its high profile approach.

Another major area of the CRC's activities was to help ethnic minority organisations in seeking funds through the community programmes of the local authority. In the 1980s the CRC assisted in the setting up of a number of community centres of one sort or another by minority ethnic communities. However, from 1986-87, it withdrew its membership from the decision making group because it believed that decisions on grant applications within the Community Programmes were increasing being made on political grounds rather than on the basis of real community needs.

Signs of Trouble and Change

Over the years, because of its strong criticism of some the Bradford Council's policies and practices, the CRC attracted a good deal of hostility from officers and elected councillors. Its activities remained under continuous public scrutiny. However, it helped the minority ethnic communities to express their demands more forcefully and boosted their confidence in dealing with the Council.

In September 1986 Bradford Council's Race Relations Advisory Committee, chaired by Mohammed Ajeeb, issued the Council's revised race relations policy document which was seriously criticised by Abdul Hameed, then chairman of the CRC. His comments on the policy erupted into an open clash between him and Graham Mahoney, Bradford Council's senior race relations officer. (T&A, 29 September and 17 December 1986)

During that August Abdul Hameed and Tim Whitfield were accused of interference in the elections of the Karmand Centre. Even though an internal investigation committee of the CRC found the allegations to be baseless and Councillor Hameed survived a vote of no confidence, the whole episode reflected very badly on the public image of the CRC. (T&A, 31 October and 11 November 1986)

It was in August 1984, during the chairmanship of Councillor Abdul Hameed, that CRC decided to withdraw its co-operation with the police for six months on the issue of the police allowing the BNP to march in the city and hold a public meeting. The ban was lifted in February 1985.

Again in September 1986, Councillor Hameed brought the CRC into controversy when he was cited as leading a march against a meeting of the Ahmadiya Muslim Association to be held in the Central Library Theatre. (T&A, 7 October 1986)

By the middle of the 1980s some serious concerns were being expressed in various quarters about the 'representative' position of the CRC. The 1986 annual meeting of the CRC Council decided to hold a wider consultation exercise with various member organisations and individuals to identify the key issues and concerns that might require immediate attention and redress. The exercise identified the following four key issues:

1. The employees and members of Bradford Council were perceived to be gradually increasing their dominance in the membership of the CRC Council and its Executive Committee. Particular reference was made to those employees of Bradford Council who had responsibilities in the race-relations field within the Council. In their case, a serious clash of interest was perceived which presented a potential danger to the 'independent identity' of the CRC and it being used to promote personal interests.
2. The disproportionate representation of 'individual members' on the Executive Committee compared with that from the 'representatives of organisations' on the CRC Council.
3. The need for the Executive Committee to reflect the membership of the CRC and the composition of the local community in relation to age, gender and ethnic origin.
4. The overall work of the organisation needed a shake up and required a greater sense of direction.

In response to these concerns the Executive Committee:
♦ Abolished the CRC panels which had large memberships of professionals from the local authority and other public sector

organisations and replaced those by seven 'issue based' working parties with memberships from outside the Executive Committee in order to guide the work of individual officers.

♦ Established a sub-committee for drawing up and monitoring the agreed annual work programme of individual officers.

♦ Established a sub-committee of the Council to deal with the problem of Council membership by 'bogus-organisations'.

Two major racial incidents in Bradford, the Bradford 12 case (1981-82) and the Salman Rushdie affair involved the CRC and had some bearing on its operation. (See chapters IV and VI for further details of these incidents)

In the year 1988-89 the publication of Salman Rushdie's book "The Satanic Verses" remained the biggest issue in the city. The CRC decided to have no particular position on the issue. This decision attracted some criticism from local Muslim organisations but the CRC argued that it was inappropriate for a secular organisation like the CRC to interfere in the affairs of a religious community and it had no intention of making any judgement on the book or its contents. However, it was deeply concerned about the profoundly damaging effects of world-wide media coverage of the reaction and activities of Bradford Muslim organisations. Despite its formally agreed position of neutrality on the issue, the CRC's role in the whole affair remained suspect in the eyes of the public and the media. Suspicion was caused by the central involvement of Dr Shabiar Akhtar, Education CRO, Ishtiaq Ahmed, Chairman of the CRC and some other prominent members of the CRC's Executive Committee in the campaign against the publication of the book albeit in their personal private capacities.

Whilst the Satanic Verses controversy was still going on, "the Gulf Crisis" came on the horizon. Some leading members of the Bradford Muslim population challenged the legitimacy of British involvement in the war and this resulted in a fierce debate about the British Muslims' 'loyalty' to Britain and the 'concept of Britishness'.

For a few years Bradford attracted a good deal of national and international attention because of the Satanic Verses and Gulf Crisis publicity. It gave the CRC (and its successor, the Bradford Racial Equality Council - BREC) a difficult race relations situation to handle because of the large Muslim population in the city and the leading role of the Bradford Council for Mosques in these incidents.

In the 1980s, the CRC started showing a serious interest in the Bradford Health Authority's employment and service provision policies and practices and tried to extend its links with it. The CRC's relations with the Bradford Health Authority were not very good. It wanted the Authority to develop a race relations policy with input from the CRC, but the Authority's response was cool and it appeared that the Authority was determined to establish its own working party on race issues without CRC's formal representation. BHA continued listening to the CRC but at the same time started establishing its own direct links with ethnic minority organisations.

1990s: Years of Change and Decline

Tim Whitfield left in December 1990 after 13 years service. He was replaced by Mohammed Naeem as Senior CRO. Bradford CRC was reconstituted as Bradford Racial Equality Council (BREC) on 10 July 1990 and as a consequence, Mohammad Naeem became Director of BREC in March 1991. The name change also resulted in revised aims and objectives of the organisation under *'New Partnership'* arrangements of the Commission for Racial Equality.

Over the years the organisation had grown in size. For instance, in 1990-91 there were 32 full and part-time staff employed in BREC and its projects. The financial systems of BREC were thoroughly examined by the local authority and changes were implemented in 1991-92. Mrs. Rubina Bhurhan became the first (Asian) woman chairperson in 1992-93. Jackie Norris, the longest serving administrative officer, retired after 23 years of service with the Council in May 1996.

A number of current and former local authority black and Asian employees who had worked as race awareness trainers continued their interest in the work of the BREC in the early part of the 1990s. Ishtiaq

Ahmed, one time chairman of the CRC Council, joined BREC as Race Equality Officer (REO) Education in 1991-92.

The 1991-92 Annual report of BREC noted its serious concern with the poor attendance at Executive Committee meetings. The report acknowledged that serious steps had to be taken to shift the focus in the work programme towards the elimination of racial discrimination, to increase the participation of women and young people and to extend the participation of all community groups. Concerns were expressed about the general waning interest in BREC across all communities. The size of the BREC Council shrank to almost half of its size in the mid-1980s. Many organisations let their membership lapse by not returning their applications forms when they came up for annual renewal. For example, in 1992-93 Council's membership dropped to 57, comprising of 41 organisations, 11 individual members and 5 associate members. Among the list of member organisations, there were 17 ethnic minority organisations, out of which 10 were Muslim organisations, one Chinese but no African or Caribbean organisations. Among the reasons for declining membership or interest in the BREC was a rapid development of direct links between minority ethnic community organisations and local institutions. Furthermore, the CRE's increasing control of the local RECs was another reason for the decline in some people's interest in joining them.

After the demise of its Educational Panel in 1986 education came firmly back on BREC's agenda in 1998. At the initiative of BREC a new LEA/BREC Education Liaison Group was established to work collaboratively on educational issues facing ethnic minority children in Bradford schools. The group worked well until the demise of BREC in March 2000.

BREC's work in the employment arena had been mainly concerned with dealing with discrimination cases brought to its notice. Because of a persistent high number of discrimination cases against Bradford Council in the early 1990s BREC repeatedly pressurised the CRE to seek injunctions against the local authority under Section 62 of the RRA 1976. In 1992-93, it assisted with 82 Industrial Tribunal cases against

The story of Bradford 1950-2002

John Haggas Plc Keighley leading to a total of 177 employment discrimination cases handled by BREC. In relation to employment issues other than actual cases of racial discrimination complaints, BREC's ability and role remained limited. BREC continued its complaint aid work in partnership with the Northern Complaint Aid Fund.

Towards the end of the 1990s BREC tried to strengthen its working links with trade unions. It had also been concerned with employment issues in the Bradford Health Authority. It played an active leading role in the setting up of Bradford Action on Health and Bradford Health & Race Equality Forum. Unemployment rates among South Asian and black young people in Bradford had been continuously 3 to 4 times higher than of white young people in the city. This has been a major concern to BREC. However it achieved very little success in this area.

In relation to its work with the Chinese community in the 1990s BREC established the West Yorkshire Chinese Community Association. It was based at the BREC offices and had a development worker who for the first time started looking into the needs of the Chinese community in the district.

A good deal of BREC's work had been reactive and ad hoc in response to local incidents. In 1992-93 it was involved in local issues such as the Mohammed Ajeeb Defence Committee, the Pakistan Relief Fund, the Ayodhia Crisis, A Week of Action on Bosnia, and a response to BBC Panorama Programme on Bradford. It was also involved in the situation arising from the Manningham riots in the summer of 1995 and the activities of the Bradford Commission established to investigate them. It became involved in Single Regeneration Budget bid applications and National Lottery grants as they came on the scene in the late 1990s. Its involvement in some of these issues was an unhelpful diversion of its limited resources from the agreed work programme.

West Yorkshire Racial Equality Council (WYREC)
In June 1994, WYREC was established as a regional REC. Its establishment had serious implications for BREC's staffing levels and work programme. At the departure of Mohammed Naeem to the WYREC, Ishtiaq Ahmed succeeded him as Director of BREC in

October 1994. His post remained the only CRE funded post after WYREC's start of operations. All other posts were local authority funded. The WYREC was folded up in November 1995 under a good deal of negative publicity, representing a disastrously failed pilot project of the CRE. As a consequence of its demise, BREC got two new officers for Employment and Racial Harassment work in 1996-97. Thus its work programme became enlarged and contained impressive new targets. New youth and racial harassment work made good progress. However this was not matched in other areas of the work programme.

Signs of Trouble Ahead
During the 1990s BREC's working approach changed significantly. The annual reports of this period present a clear view of the changes.

♦ BREC now had an annual Working Programme agreed by its Work Programme Sub-committee and approved by the CRE as a condition of continued grant aid support. It was a step towards bringing discipline, clear direction and measurable achievements into the work of the individual officers as well as the organisation as a whole. However, the necessity to set measurable targets in each area of work led to a tendency to sacrifice substance in the pursuit of impressive statistics. This led the officers to concentrate on committee work and attendance at meetings with other organisations. This resulted in a gradual decline in quantifiable tangible achievements other than in areas of individual casework. The officers became more concerned to produce nicely worded accounts of their work and achievements even to the point of over-emphasising the importance of the issues addressed. The annual reports became over-filled with commentary on the nature and magnitude of problems and issues related to the work of BREC rather than with the achievement of work programme targets. Following this general trend the annual reports became glossier, graphic in presentation of facts, but thinner in real contents. The introduction of work programmes did introduce planning and target setting into the activities of officers, however the second function of the work programme, as a monitoring tool, was rarely used in an effective way by the Executive Committee.

♦ The 1990s present a clear indication of BREC's working in collaboration and partnership with other organisations on similar issues, a healthy change in the use of limited human resources through avoiding duplication of work in the same field. Despite its involvement in the Inter-Agency Domestic Violence / Asian Women's Group and continuing the multi-agency approach to racial harassment cases with the police and the local authority, the impression was growing of BREC as a declining organisation, looking for a role.

♦ BREC's approach to working with other organisations and local institutions became rather aggressive, critical and confrontational. This indicated a shift from a "promotional" strategy to an "implementation" approach. Most institutions, particularly the local authority, were resentful of the manner in which they were criticised for their failings in achieving equality of opportunity. A more supportive role in addressing the areas of identified concern would have presented a better image of BREC and earned its officers more respect and acceptance than the overtly 'negative approach' they appeared to have adopted.

♦ Over the years there had been a clear polarisation in membership of the BREC Council. A large number of 'white organisations' and 'white individual members' either left the Council or showed little interest in its activities. The attendance at Council meetings shrank to small numbers of the same committed people. Serious concern arose about the poor attendance at the Executive Committee meetings too. The organisation's efforts to increase the participation of young people, women and African and Caribbean community members had very little impact.

♦ At the same time the size of the organisation grew in terms of staff and the number of projects it was handling. There were increased external pressures particularly from the CRE for working to the agreed programme and for meeting the approved targets. However, it was becoming increasing evident that not all the staff had the ability, skills and training to cope with the new demands of the jobs they were doing, resulting in long periods of sickness for some

members. Despite support and gentle pressure from the Executive
Committee they did not appear to be working to their full potential.

♦ The work culture in the office had become casual, sloppy and
loosely co-ordinated. There were clear symptoms of staff
inefficiency. The papers for meetings were generally sent out late,
more and more papers were tabled at the meetings and meetings
were cancelled fairly regularly on the pretext of lack of business.
Assurances from the Director of improvements in the situation were
not delivered.

♦ Over the period the strict scrutiny of finances and accountability had
reduced. The presentation of accounts to the Executive Committee
had lost regularity. For example none of the annual reports of the
1990s contain a copy of the financial accounts. At times, they were
not even circulated at the annual general meetings.

♦ Nevertheless, the Executive Committee must share the
responsibility for not performing its duty in providing effective
governance. Over the years the waning enthusiasm within the
Council to seek election to the Executive Committee resulted in the
continuation of the same people year after year. From the lack of
contributions to the business at meetings by some members it was
apparent that they had no real interest in the running of the
organisation beyond the maintenance of their own status and
position. Therefore, the Executive Committee's own inadequacies
and lack of firm commitment to the monitoring of the operation of
the organisation and the performance of individual officers allowed
the inefficiencies to grow from bad to worst.

♦ Relations between the staff and the honorary officers of BREC gave
the impression of a "social club environment" making it difficult for
them to introduce and monitor effective management and
governance. The national review of the CRCs in the 1990s stressed
that the most regular problem in the working of CRCs stemmed
from bad management by voluntary committees or from the lack of
professionalism by CROs. The review tried to redress the issues by

giving professionals the central role and responsibility for the management affairs of the reconstituted RECs. Sadly, despite the training provided to the REOs, not many of them developed a professional approach to their work and many of them seriously lacked management skills. Therefore, the situation in Bradford did not seem in any way different from many other RECs.

♦ Cordial relations between the officials and the voluntary office bearers can be a strength for organisations and thus desirable. But, here the problem was that the elected key officers allowed the fine balance between their governance responsibilities and cordial supporting role towards officers, to slip to the level of close personal friendships. Such a situation made it difficult to ask searching questions when things were not going right. Even those individuals who had serious concerns about the inefficient management were reluctant to speak out from the fear of being singled out. This was very much the situation at BREC for a number of years.

♦ Locally the West Yorkshire Race Equality Council was confused with the BREC as they shared premises and was headed by the other's former director. The circumstances surrounding the early collapse of the WYREC reflected badly on the image of the BREC too. Some of the media reports about the failure of the WYREC confused it with the BREC, thus denting the latter's credibility and damaging its public image. Despite the strenuous efforts of its new Director, BREC found it difficult to gain the confidence of communities across the board.

♦ The Muslim dominance in BREC staff sent out signals of its lack of "denominational independence" and its being "an organisation of all" and "an organisation for all". Among the three trustees, two were Muslim and one white. Despite the fact that Ishtiaq Ahmed was an able hard working professional with a keen strategic approach to establishing inter-community relations and alliances across cultural, national and religious divides, he was not fully successful in projecting an image of being secular and neutral. He was perceived more as a Muslim representative and a supporter of Muslim causes because of his previous close associations with the

The struggle for racial justice

Islamic Youth Movement (in the 1970s) and the Bradford Council for Mosques (in the 1990s). According to Lewis (1994, p 147) the CRC served two functions for Muslims in Bradford. First, it served as a nursery for Muslim politicians, where the necessary skills, confidence and contacts were developed. For instance, five Muslim councillors were active members of the CRC in the 1980s. Second, the CRC was the main forum where officers of the Council for Mosques and Muslim councillors met and where support for Muslim concerns in the wider community could be tested. The overlapping membership of the Muslim councillors, between their membership of the Council of Mosques and the CRC was causing serious concern to the representatives of other minority communities represented on the CRC. Particularly the Hindus in the city were publicly critical of the CRC's preoccupation and positive bias towards Muslim concerns and the consequent alienation of other minority communities from its activities and participation.

♦ The *Bradford Commission Report* on the Manningham race disturbances in 1995 were highly critical of the role and achievements of the BREC. The main report stated that *"it is now seen as part of the establishment, its role and potential is undervalued" by many of the younger people and it did not command the confidence of the African Caribbean community. It further stated that "whilst it clearly could have a role to play as an inter-agency facilitator, the REC does not currently influence mainstream activities in the city significantly." (The Bradford Commission Report, 1996, page 99).*

♦ The alternative report on the Manningham riots by M Taj, *A 'Can Do' City,* was highly appreciative of the CRC's contributions in "promoting understanding between Bradford's various communities" and its potential role in the "consideration and expression of common concerns unmediated by religious, national and sectional loyalties". At the same time it noted that *"the Council for Racial Equality has not become the force for positive change that it once promised to be. It runs a continual risk of being marginalised by more contentious issues and more strident voices.*

Moreover, its activities have been far more re-active than pro-active, it has become too associated with complaint than pre-emption, too concerned with reflection than analysis."

♦ Responding to these criticisms *'Racial Equality Council's Response to Bradford Commission Report'* (an undated paper presented to the Executive Committee by BREC's Director) suggested that such comments were "due to the lack of understanding of the work of the Bradford Racial Equality Council on the part of the Commissioners."

Final Collapse: 1999-2000

For the year 1998-99, Lynne Kent, the first white woman, was unanimously elected Chairman of the BREC under an agreed strategic decision between a number of senior members of the Executive Committee. Mrs Kent's election was intended to recapture the interest of white community members in the work of the Council and more importantly to change the work culture within BREC which was felt to be dominated by some Muslim male officers. It was recognized that the organisation lacked gender equality. Despite tremendous support from the Executive Committee, the previous Asian woman chairman, Mrs Rubina Bhurhan (1992-1993), had had an uneasy time attempting to bring efficiency, equality and professionalism into the working of BREC.

Three major incidents at the BREC led it to its eventual demise. The first incident relates to an investigation of its financial records. The troubles started with the swoop on the BREC offices by the auditors, KPMG, on 8 March 1999, seizing its files for investigation. One officer was accused of misappropriation of BREC's funds. The officer concerned was suspended in April and after a disciplinary hearing he was dismissed in November. The case was reported to the police for a further criminal investigation.

The second incident related to the complaints of Ms Nadia Habashi, a female officer of the BREC. These were of indecent assault and sex discrimination directed against Ishtiaq Ahmed, Director of the BREC. He was arrested on 11 March 1999 and questioned by the police over the complaint of indecent assault. However, the police dropped the charges. A newly formed group, Action for Racial Justice, publicly supported the Director. On 27 August Ms Habashi began her Employment Tribunal case claiming unlawful sex discrimination under the Sex Discrimination Act 1975 by two officers of the BREC. The tribunal gave its decision on 2 November. Saleem Sharif who had been earlier dismissed as a result of the internal investigation by the BREC was found to have unlawfully discriminated against Ms Habashi by asking her to clean the office and make tea and coffee for a staff meeting. Ishtiaq Ahmed, the Director of the BREC, was judged to have unlawfully discriminated against her by way of victimisation when he extended her probationary period. However, the tribunal dismissed her case of indecent assault against the Director.

The third incident was a case of racial discrimination against BREC by a white female office worker, Liz King, with a service of 18 years at the BREC. The case was finally settled out of court in December 1999.

In view of the investigation into alleged financial irregularities at the BREC, the Lottery Charities Board froze its £100,000 grant for the project Bradford Alliance Against Racial Harassment (BAARH). As a consequence of the tribunal decision the CRE gave a second blow to the BREC by withdrawing its annual grant of £75,000 that paid the salaries of three officers of the BREC, including the salary of its Director. The decisions of these two major funding organisations created a serious dilemma for Bradford Council as to whether to carry on providing its own £200,000 grant to an organisation that appeared to have lost its credibility. The BREC was now in complete turmoil and Bradford Council wanted a response from it about the action it would take to meet with its financial crisis.

In a written communication with the author, Ishtiaq Ahmed, Director of BREC, gave a different and additional set of reasons and perspectives for the hostile approach of the LA and the CRE towards the BREC. He admitted that some mistakes may have been made or that things could have been done to avoid the BREC's crisis. However, he firmly believed that no other organisation would have suffered the same fate (at the hands of the BREC's funders) because a few of its staff had been out of line. He suggested that there was another side to the official deliberations and formal adopted positions. **He asserted that**:

1. *The BREC's high profile and scathing criticism of the police and indirectly of the local authority at the Stephen Lawrence Enquiry became a major source of embarrassment to both institutions and the race relations in the city.*

2. *BREC's support and successful winning of Mohammad Masood's case of discrimination against Bradford Council which had implicated some of the senior officers of the Council and political leaders also angered officers and politicians alike. Again BREC was becoming a liability. No officer of the Council was suspended or disciplined following this case and some of those involved had since been promoted. This doesn't say much for the Council's need for probity. The local CAB had allegations of discrimination against it, was experiencing serious financial problems, had officers suspended because of inter-staff strife and rivalries, had the management committee continuously complaining about not being involved and in crisis, yet elected members and officers kept it hushed up and the CAB continued to receive the same level of support.*

3. *A number of Asian politicians had been incensed by his criticism of their role within party political machinery at a public meeting organised by the Action for Racial Justice. These politicians saw an opportunity to teach him a lesson. According to them he was becoming too big for his shoes. This explained their distance from the BREC's difficulties and the silent encouragement which they provided for the eventual shutdown of the organisation. All this was not conjecture on his part but that had been said to him or communicated to him.*

4. *There was a strongly held belief amongst the local Labour leadership that the BREC was increasingly becoming a platform for the Asian conservatives. There was a malicious rumour that he had also gone Tory.*

5. *There was a deliberate attempt to project the BREC as a Muslim dominated organisation despite the fact that the Executive*

Committee was predominantly non-Muslim and for a part of the 1990s the chairs and key honorary officers were non-Muslims. Unfortunately, some of the Executive members were also in the forefront of this propaganda.

6. *The local CRE Commissioner had personally vowed to shut the local BREC because of his personal clashes with members of the staff and the refusal of the staff to jump to his personal dictates. The CRE and the Chief Executive were aware of this yet the same Commissioner was involved in deciding the future of the BREC.*

As a consequence of the Lottery Grant being frozen and the CRE's grant finishing at the end of December 1999, all seventeen of BREC's employees were issued with redundancy notices. A public meeting of mainly black and Asian people concerned about the future of race relations work in the city and the loss of seventeen jobs expressed their determination to campaign to save the BREC.

It was widely believed that Bradford Council expected the BREC to terminate the services of its Director. However, the BREC's Executive Committee was proposing immediately to establish a panel from its Personnel Sub-committee to assess the performance of the Director. And at the same time to set up a group composed of some of the members of BREC, one representative from the CRE, one member of Bradford Council and the BREC Trustees, to review the role of the BREC.

On 2 December 1999, the Executive Committee held a meeting with the Chief Executive of Bradford Council, Ian Stewart, and the Leader of the Council, Ian Greenwood, to discuss its proposal. Without clearly articulating their expectations, both Ian Greenwood and Ian Stewart were not ready to accept the proposal to safeguard the future of the BREC. They argued that an organisation with a duty to work towards achieving "equality" found guilty of sex discrimination against its own employee, and being currently investigated for alleged financial irregularities, no longer remained a credible and a viable organisation to carry out race relations work in the city. At least not in its present form.

Then and there after a brief private meeting the Executive Committee members unanimously took the decision to resign on block.

The full Council at its meeting on 6 December 1999 approved the resignation decision of the Executive Committee. The Council appointed an interim committee of three persons, Liaquat Hussain, Ken Fabian and Ms Mollie Summerville (Chairman) to work with the two trustees Sher Azam and the Right Reverend, David Smith, Bishop of Bradford to work out the future of the Council. Ken Fabian resigned from this committee soon afterwards for personal reasons.

After failing to reach any acceptable compromises with the three funding organisations and facing a continually increasing financial deficit, the Trustees and the Interim Committee decided to close the organisation. On 24 February 2000, the Oak Lane offices of the BREC were boarded up, its employees were relieved of their duties and the office contents were deposited with Bradford Council for safe custody.

On 23 March 2000 BREC held a special meeting at the Carlisle Business Centre to consider a resolution to close down its operation and to dissolve the organisation as of that day. Out of 25 members present 21 voted for its closure (with one abstention and one 'no' vote). This decision closed all the three parts of BREC: Bradford REC, Keighley branch of REC and Project Comtran. The meeting also appointed Ken Fortune of Horwath Clark Whitehill (Chartered Accountants) to act as liquidator.

BREC's Contribution to Race Relations
In the late 1990s BREC attracted a significant amount of criticism from a number of quarters. Nevertheless, its record of positive contributions to the life of minority ethnic communities in Bradford is impressive. Its tireless efforts to develop good relations between diverse communities over a period of 33 years are praiseworthy. It also deserves credit and public recognition for its persistent endeavours to encourage, cajole and support local institutions to create policies, procedures and practices for providing equality of opportunity to all the citizens of Bradford. Being critical of those who, at times, were failing to make their required or potential contribution in the development of a fair and just society, was

its duty. According to Ahmed (1997) the BREC has contributed to the life of Bradford by:

1. *Bringing together various sections of the community on the issues of race relations and providing more opportunities for a focused debate on the issue of race relations.*
2. *Facilitating the development of the Asian and black voluntary sector.*
3. *Challenging discrimination through providing direct help to victims of discrimination and developing racial equality programmes within private and public sector bodies.*

The other major contribution of the BREC had been to act as an intermediary between ethnic minority communities and local institutions, organisations and agencies in dealing with the difficulties they faced in serving their Asian and black clients / employees on equal terms.

For minority ethnic communities, particularly the Pakistani and Bangladeshi communities in Bradford and Keighley, BREC was the major advice agency in dealing with their immigration, citizenship and welfare problems.

It is also interesting to note that a number of individuals associated with the CRC / BREC over the years moved into important positions locally and nationally. (1) The achievements of these individuals provides clear evidence that BREC and its predecessors have served many individuals from the minority ethnic communities in building their confidence and giving them the experience which would enable them to move into positions of status and influence. From the minority ethnic communities' standpoint this is a highly significant contribution, as these individuals also act as successful role models. A full list of honorary officers who served the CRC/BREC is included in Appendix A as a tribute to their contributions to the community relations in the city.

The story of Bradford 1950-2002

Most of the work of the BCCCI and its successors CRC /BREC was carried out by a number of different panels set up to cover education, health, housing, employment, youth and matrimonial cases. Some of these panels worked very effectively and had a significant impact on the policies and practices of major service providers; whilst others remained simply forums for exchanges of views and concerns by like-minded professionals. These panels proved extremely useful: (a) in involving large numbers of individuals in the general work of the CRC, and (b) in providing a platform for like minded individuals to share common difficulties, concerns, issues, frustrations as well as good practice in areas of their particular professional interests. These panels were formally disbanded in 1986 to be replaced by some small groups giving advice and support to individual officers in their activities. The new arrangement was not only slow to start, it just did not work. Its failure denied the officers access to the most valuable community-based voluntary professional resource and support. As a consequence of the change the organisation became inward looking.

The most effective of the panels was the **Education Panel** set up in 1968. (2) During the 1970s the work of the Panel was largely focused on:

♦ Regular meetings with the parents of children of Commonwealth immigrants about the schooling system in the city, problems their children faced in schools and parental rights in education. The Panel also produced leaflets in community languages on these topics.
♦ The organisation of multi-racial playgroups in school summer holidays during the period 1972-75.
♦ Giving talks in schools on South Asian cultures, religions and the educational systems of the Indian Sub-continent in order to develop local teachers' understanding of the difficulties Asian children were facing in Bradford.
♦ Taking initiatives in the field of teaching English to the new arrivals. It organised projects involving Sixth Formers from local schools teaching English to Asian children. The Panel pioneered a scheme of teaching English to men and women at home by volunteers, which was formally taken over by the Local Education Authority under its Home Tutoring Scheme.

The struggle for racial justice

- ◆ Establishing youth clubs for Asian youngsters in 1967 and 1969; however without much success.
- ◆ Regular speaking engagements at conferences, church meetings, meetings in schools and colleges in the area by Panel chairs and the Education CRO. The Panel organised two successful conferences on the Asian cultures in the city.
- ◆ Dealing with concerns about the Bussing Policy of the LEA and the issues of mother tongue teaching (community languages).

Towards the end of the 1970s and particularly at the beginning of the 1980s the educational issues in Bradford took a different turn. Over the years the CRC had been involved in the campaign against the Bussing Policy of the LEA. A major change in the provision of education for immigrant children came with the abolition of this policy. An investigation by the Commission for Racial Equality in 1979 found the policy to be racially discriminatory. The LEA agreed to phase out the policy between 1980-84.

In the early 1980s Bradford Council started developing and experimenting with a concept of multi-cultural education. The Education Panel of the CRC became a major forum for discussing general issues concerning mother-tongue teaching, allocation of school places, extended holidays in the sub-continent and the provision of halal meat in schools. The panel worked with ethnic minority parents to enhance their awareness and understanding of their rights and responsibilities in relation to the education of their children. Its activities helped in boosting the confidence of parents in 'parent power'. For example, an Asian parents meeting organised by the panel in Drummond school in 1981was able to put on hold a proposal of the LEA to take away the guarantee of a place in the same school to children returning after more than six weeks absence abroad. The panel was also successful in persuading the LEA to publish leaflets in community languages about its policy and provision for the education of ethnic minority children.

The Education Panel became a major contributor to the development and discussion of the Local Administrative Memoranda of the LEA on ethnic minority pupils in schools. It also contributed significantly to the LEA's development of multicultural education policies and curriculum. 1983-84 became a year of major educational issues that included:

- The introduction of a new agreed syllabus of religious education in schools.

- The introduction of halal meat in Bradford schools that attracted considerable opposition from Animal Rights groups.

- The Muslim Parents Association's proposal to take over five Bradford schools that generated a major debate on the issue of religious and single sex schools.

- The proposal to merge BelleVue Boys and Girls schools thus abolishing the existence of the only single sex schools in the LEA control.

- The introduction of a Local Authority Memorandum on racial harassment attracted considerable opposition from head-teachers.

- The Honeyford affair remained the focus of the Panel's activities for over two years. Some members of the Panel were referred to in the Honeyford's controversial articles. In the Honeyford saga the CRC supported the Drummond Parents Action Group and they remained active partners m the campaign for his removal and the public demonstrations and press publicity against his views on multi-cultural education and denigration of Asian cultures. Local politicians took sharply divided positions on his views and the action to be taken against him. After a considerable lapse of time and fierce debates, the Education Committee of the LEA passed a resolution of no confidence in him. Eventually, in 1985, he took early retirement.

After the Educational Panel was formally closed down in 1986 education came firmly back on BREC's agenda in 1998. At the initiative of the BREC a new LEA/BREC Education Liaison Group was established to work collaboratively on the educational issues facing ethnic minority children in Bradford schools. In the brief period before the demise of BREC in March 2000, the liaison group met about six times and had useful discussions which identified the following issues of mutual concern.

➤ Section 11 Funding arrangements had been an issue of continuous interest to BREC and despite BREC being critical about the less than effective use of funds it became centrally involved in the campaign to save Section 11 funding for the city in 1997/98.
➤ The increase of incidents of racial harassment in schools.
➤ Over the years the number of appointments of Asian and black school governors has increased from 60 in 1990-91 to 300 in 1993-94 but the relatively low numbers and a declining interest in the appointment of more governors from the minority communities remains a matter of concern.
➤ The expulsion and exclusion of children from schools has become an issue for Pakistani parents in particular.
➤ It became firmly established that Bradford faced a serious situation of under-achievement particularly amongst children of Pakistani and Bangladeshi origin.
➤ Bangladeshi and Pakistani parents had been highly critical of procedures for the allocation of school places. Bangladeshi parents unsuccessfully sought a judicial review of these procedures in 1993. An appeal lodged against the court decision was also lost at the High Court. However these concerns persist.

Bradford CRC established its **Employment Panel** in 1968. Despite a number of serious attempts the Panel failed to create any sustained interest or enthusiasm among local employers and trade unions in its work or in its attempts to persuade them to join the Panel. Despite the presence of serious problems about the poor relations between white and black / Asian employees at shop-floor level, discrimination in employment and exceptionally high rates of unemployment among Asian school leavers, local employers and trade unions were reluctant to acknowledge that these were significant issues. For example, local banks and building societies in the city had no black or Asian faces in their workforce even in the early 1970s but were not ready to accept the CRC's concern about it. Nevertheless, local employers regularly called the CRC officers for advice and support in resolving problems concerning the employment of Asian workers. Only a few of them, such as Thomas Burnley & Sons Ltd. in Gomersal and Brackendale Mills in Thackley, arranged CRC-supported cultural awareness courses for their managers and supervisors. In 1975, in sheer frustration, the Panel decided to suspend its activities. It was revived in 1979 and remained in existence until 1987. (3)

Health and Welfare Panel was started as an Advisory / Matrimonial Panel to deal with an increasing number of domestic problems arising from the re-union of South Asian families and especially concerning young South Asian girls growing up in Bradford. After a year or so it was taken over by George Moore, a senior officer of the Probation Service. Its role was widened beyond domestic issues to deal with all sorts of other problems relating to black and Asian involvement in areas of the criminal justice system, particularly the courts. As a consequence, the CRC set up a new health and welfare panel to deal with problems in areas such as health and social services.

In its new form the panel continued to work reasonably well for almost 12 years. For the most part the Panel was chaired by doctors who used the Panel to raise the awareness of many colleagues and professionals about the particular health and welfare issues facing blacks and Asians in the city. (4) Mr. N S Farrar (1982-85) during his chairmanship shifted the focus of its activities to concentrate upon issues relating to black and Asian patients and social services' clients from minority communities.

Over the years, social, health and welfare issues facing the service providers and the professionals working in these fields in the city dominated the business of the Panel. Black and Asian clients own perspectives on such issues were only marginally represented in its discussions. Some regular agenda items for discussion at the panel meetings included:
- Rickets and the osteomalacia problem
- Homeless women and girls / refuge houses for Asian women and girls
- Fostering and adoption
- Problems in hospitals
- Polygamous marriages
- Asian girls molested outside schools

The struggle for racial justice

CRC/BREC worked with the police through its **Police Liaison Panel**. Its relations with the local police were always variable. With John Naylor's professional police background he usually found it easy and comfortable to approach the police with regard to individual problems or incidents. However, his efforts to establish some sort of formal stable arrangements to discuss day to day issues as they emerged, and to work towards developing continued long-term good relations between the police and the minority communities had little success. The approach of the Police Community Affairs officers was limited to the consultation or involvement of CRC staff or minority ethnic community leaders in resolving individual problems as and when they arose. They were also used to provide some input into police community relations and cultural awareness courses - usually run at the Police Academy in Wakefield.

The Scarman Report (1981) on the race riots in Brixton, Moss Side, Chapletown in Leeds and elsewhere in Britain in 1981 recommended changes in police training. In response to this recommendation a Police Liaison Panel was established in Bradford to improve links between the police, the CRC and the minority ethnic communities. As a part of its commitment, the CRC provided regular inputs into cultural and racism awareness courses arranged by the police.

The CRC's participation in the activities of the Panel was generally educational, cautionary and mildly critical. But it was never hard hitting or challenging to the presence of wide spread racism among police officers at all levels. This low key promotional role did help to maintain good working relationship with the police but did not have any serious impact on the prevailing racist culture of the police. John Naylor's successor, Tim Whitfield, who had worked in the probation service, was willing to challenge police racism. However his attempts generally met with resentment.

In 1984-85 relations between the CRC and the police completely broke down for a while. This was due to the incident when the police allowed the British National Party to organise a march in the city and to hold a public meeting without any liaison with the CRC. As a consequence of this, the CRC decided on a policy of no cooperation with the police for six months until February 1985. (5)

In the 1990s the working relations between the CRC and the police remained cordial but casual and semi-formal. It was only a short while before the demise of the BREC in March 2000 that a fresh formal link in the form of a Liaison Group was established. Unfortunately, it had an extremely short life.

With the recession and decline of textiles unemployment particularly among South Asian school- leavers became a significant issue and a lot more cases of discrimination in employment started coming forward. The CRC set up a training workshop to alleviate the problem. **Manningham Workshop** was established with funding from the Manpower Services Commission under the general guidance of an advisory committee. The Workshop employed six staff and offered courses in woodwork and screen-printing. The Workshop's policy, procedures and management remained a continuous matter of concern for the Executive Committee and the CRC/BREC never felt that it had proper control of it. It was a relief for the BREC when it finally relinquished responsibility for the Workshop in 1991-92.

Since the early 1990s BREC managed **Project Comtran**. The project was set up as a limited company and employed three staff. Its funding came from the Local Authority, Bradford TEC and Section 11 Grants etc. Its funding position was always insecure. It provided training to unemployed workers from ethnic minority communities offering courses in computing and computers, counselling, communication, self-development, business development, foundation community development and language translation courses accredited by the Institute of Linguistics. It also ran some short courses in collaboration with the Open University in Leeds. The Open College Network and Bradford College accredited some of its courses. It was recognised that it should run courses under the Positive Action section of the RRA 1976. It also ran a Pre-Diploma in Social Work course in partnership with Bradford Social Services Training Unit. On the whole, despite the diversity in its training provision, the project had a qualified success.

The struggle for racial justice

Bradford Racial Equality Council Office
Photograph by kind permission of the T&A, Bradford

12

RACE RELATIONS APPROACH AND POLICIES OF BRADFORD COUNCIL

No Problems Here—No Policy

Bradford Council had no specific race relations policy until the beginning of the 1980s. Bradford has a long established tradition of receiving immigrants from different countries such as Ireland, Germany and many eastern European countries. However, from the 1950s the major immigration into Bradford had been from the Indian sub-continent and the West Indies. The background of these immigrants from New Commonwealth countries was distinctively different from those of the earlier immigrants who were largely white Europeans. The new arrivals from the early 1950s:

- had black or brown skin colour;
- were mostly male on short term earning trips;
- had, in most cases, little knowledge of the English language or western cultural traditions; and
- had their own strongly distinctive cultural, religious and linguistic identities.

These elements of "foreignness" made them easy targets for discrimination and prejudice. There was a strong local as well as national anti-immigration political rhetoric. Some highly articulate right-wing politicians and leaders of trade unions were hostile towards immigrants on the basis of the widespread belief that the continuous waves of newcomers were taking their jobs, keeping wages low and impeding the rise of ordinary citizens' living standards. It was suggested, without much evidence, that immigrants were making excessive demands on social services such as health, education and welfare. Nationally, the extreme right parties such as the National Front and the British National Party and at the local level the Yorkshire Stop Immigration Campaign, led by Wibsey Conservative councillor, Jim Merrick, continued to stir up hatred against the immigrants arguing that they were spreading diseases and building their numbers through illegal

The struggle for racial justice

immigration and very high fertility rates. The growing concentration of 'black' immigrants in large numbers in inner-city locations, with distinctively different cultures, languages and religious beliefs and practices, was seen as a serious threat to community relations and traditional ways of life. Their presence was perceived as a danger to peaceful co-existence and a new challenge for authorities to maintain stability in urban life. Such exaggerated myths ignored the fact that new immigrants were an economic necessity and a valuable ready pool of 'human capital'.

These immigrant groups had little interaction between one another. They worked and settled almost in isolation from the local white communities. Public sector institutions and bodies worked on the assumption that over a period of time their 'newness' would fade if not totally disappear and they would 'integrate / assimilate' like their predecessors. Ironically even those who came to the city from Eastern European countries after the World War II and who were themselves still relatively isolated, had their own clubs and language teaching schools and were themselves facing serious disadvantage, added their support to this view. Letters from people of Polish, Ukrainian and Yugoslavian origin appeared in the Telegraph & Argus claiming that they had used a 'self-help' approach to resolving their difficulties in settling in and meeting their special needs rather than expecting the authorities to make changes based on linguistic or cultural differences.

With the joining of male immigrants by their families in the 1960s and 1970s the 'myth of return' was shattered, and South Asian social infrastructures in the inner-city areas became firmly established. New communities emerged around religious groupings with their own social structures based on extended families and the *'biradari'* system. Their strong preferences and efforts for 'cultural maintenance' put a big question mark on the official approach of 'no separate race-relation or social policy' in dealing with the specific educational, health, housing or social services issues arising from the presence of South Asian and Afro-Caribbean communities in the city. The need for the adoption of new measures to meet their special requirements or to take specific initiatives to deal with their 'social deprivation' or 'racial disadvantage' was considered unnecessary and politically unacceptable as an example of privileged treatment. Most of Bradford Council's services, like the services of most other authorities, remained 'ethnocentric' dealing with new communities' needs as 'problems' for resolution with ad-hoc solutions.

Despite some quiet murmurs, latent discontentment, occasional incidents of public expressions against racial discrimination and prejudice, 'immigrant' communities did not protest strongly enough to engender sufficient concern amongst politicians to acknowledge the presence of 'widely pervasive racism'. They also exhibited great reluctance in making demands for meeting their culture / religion specific needs or even asking for parity or equality of treatment in normal service provision. Obviously, it was a deliberate approach of 'keeping their heads down', more than anything else, in order to avoid further resentment by the local white population.

Everything Wasn't Right--A Policy Was Needed

By the 1980s, immigration from the New Commonwealth had been strictly limited and controlled. Some significant national and local studies had firmly established the facts of racial discrimination and disadvantage in Britain, strong anti-discrimination legislation was in place to deal with race-related issues, and the ethnic minority communities had matured and become politically confident enough to challenge the presence of 'institutional racism'. The relevance of sociological concepts such as assimilation, integration and pluralism that were used to support the development of social policies were widely debated and replaced by new concepts of 'equal opportunity' and 'multiculturalism'.

In 1981 a report on the state of race relations in the city, *The Turning Points: A Review of Race Relations in Bradford* was produced for Bradford Council's Management Team. This review was carried out partly under pressure from the Commission for Racial Equality and partly for the practical purpose of securing Section 11 funding from the Government. The ethnic minority communities' concerns around inequality in the provision of services; a rapidly increasing second generation of South Asians having different expectations to those of their parents'; and the rise of right-wing political forces both nationally and in Bradford were further factors making such a review an urgent necessity. The report stressed that "race relations in Bradford were very quickly approaching a turning point".

The report noted that the distinctive feature of the Bradford community was
> *"the relative size and confidence and the large growing dominance of its Pakistani and Muslim character. But it is of course precisely this dominance which defines the special character of race relations in Bradford. For, of all immigrant groups, Pakistanis appear the most anxious to maintain their links with their societies of origin; and of all imported religions, Islam-particularly in its expansive mood –appears the most insistent in its demands for separation, and the maintenance of cultural standards."* (1)

This report makes interesting reading. On the one hand, it attempts to defend the local authority's approach so far in dealing with the 'problems' of new immigrants as being practical and based on the historical experience of dealing with earlier immigrations into the city. The report claimed that

> *"much of what has been done in Bradford over the recent years has been in the forefront of national practice and in many respects the Council has a record it can be proud of, and indeed one which the CRE would wish other authorities to emulate".*

On the other hand, its stark conclusion that "the Council does not always know what it is doing, does not always know why, and does not have the machinery to know when it should change what it is doing" was absolutely damning. The report identified the following particular weaknesses in the Council's approach. That the Council had:

> *no "appropriate" arrangements to initiate, let alone monitor, policy on racial matters;*

The story of Bradford 1950-2002

*policies which emerged, pragmatically on a strictly ad hoc
basis, always at the margin, and nearly always at the
"fieldwork" or "practitioner" level;
never given any consideration to race relations as "ethnic
development";
Seldom identified racial disadvantage as an issue in its own
right; and
no procedure in existence to ensure that the special needs of the
ethnic minorities emerged, other than by accident, when matters
affecting them were discussed and decided.*

"What the Council was doing" was not seen to be a matter of concern by
the authors of the report but they were concerned about "how it [the
Council] sets about doing it. The report argued that "there may well
have been once a reasonable justification for this manner of operation
and policy making". Justification was largely based on the fact that
Asian numbers were relatively small, contact with the host community
minimal, and demands made on the Council's services correspondingly
low, except in the case of education. The 'inactivity' on the part of the
Council was also based on the unrealistic belief that the Asians will help
themselves anyway, and in due course of time they too would assimilate
in the natural processes of adjustment. The situation of race relations
was perceived to be in accordance with the new immigrant
"community's own preferences".

The apparent 'good race relations' were largely due to the new comers
simply using the spare capacity in the labour market and cheap housing
without competing with the white population and thus avoiding conflict.
Socially, the new communities and the local population were two
separate worlds existing side by side without many interactions.
Therefore, 'good race relations' basically meant 'no race relations'.

The report questioned the relevance of these justifications and pointed
out that it was no longer reasonable to leave policy making to chance
and it was becoming increasingly dangerous to maintain 'race' as a
subject of taboo. Despite this blunt warning about the changed situation
the report showed great reluctance in admitting the extent of racial
prejudice, white hostility and race discrimination in the city. However,

111

the report identified some serious weaknesses in the Council's approach and suggested changes.

The report briefly examined the situation in four areas: employment, education, housing and social services. Up to the 1980s housing had never been perceived as a 'real racial' issue in Bradford. It was stressed that 'indirect discrimination' rather than 'direct discrimination' might be a problem. However, Asian housing conditions had reached a turning point for a variety of reasons, including the shortage of cheap properties in the inner city areas in relations to a rapid increase in demand by South Asian young people trying to establish their independent households. Capital investment in the housing sector was low and the economic power of Asians was declining due to their rising rates of unemployment.

Locally, employment was another area like housing where racial discrimination was seen as individual incidents of direct and indirect discrimination until Asians started losing jobs at a faster rate due to the restructuring in the local labour market arising from a sharp decline in textile, manufacturing and transport jobs. Unemployment became a major local concern when young South Asians started coming into the labour market in growing numbers.

In the light of its findings the authors of the report recommended that there was an urgent need for a policy statement, the creation of machinery for its implementation and the establishment of a "lead Committee" to oversee the development of race relations work within the Council. This report became the basis for the Council's first Race Relations Policy Statement in 1981.

Race Relations Policy Statement 1981

After the passing of the Race Relations Act 1976 (RRA), officers of the newly established CRE visited Bradford in 1977 and held a high profile meeting with senior politicians, local authority officers and some prominent community leaders. The then Chief Executive of the Council, Gordon Moore, partly under pressure from the CRE and partly due to his personal commitment to good community relations, showed his determination for a radical change in dealing with race related issues in the city. Some politicians' unqualified support encouraged him to adopt a high profile approach to bring about a change in the manner of developing policies and the way the provision of services was meeting the needs of ethnic minority groups in the city.

The publication of *District Trends* (starting with the 1979 issue) established some hard facts about the position of ethnic minority communities in the city and the nature and magnitude of racial disadvantage from which they were suffering. These documents had a major impact on the development of the Council's policies particularly in employment, education and housing.

RRA 1976 was put into place in 1976, however, it took 5 years for Bradford to issue its first race relations policy statement and to adopt a plan of action. Even this action was taken in the wake of race riots that occurred in the summer of 1981in some of Britain's major cities. Bradford fortunately escaped such public disturbances but experienced the impact of the "Bradford 12" case as explained earlier in chapter IV. Those incidents sent a clear message that Bradford might also be sitting on a time bomb.

The Council issued its first race relations policy statement, *Race Relations: The 12 Point Plan* (See Appendix B1) the preamble of which read:

> *"Bradford Council pledges itself to take all necessary steps as a major employer, provider of services and influence on public opinion to improve race relations in our city.*
> *We commit ourselves to encouraging equal opportunities and fighting both racial discrimination and racial disadvantage with positive action now.*
> *We also recognise we are a multi-racial, multi-cultural city and that every section of the community has an equal right to maintain its own identity, culture, language, religion and customs.*
> *We believe these ties of culture and ethnic loyalty are an asset to Bradford and we promise to take them into account in planning our services."*

As a part of the policy the Council set up the Race Relations Advisory Group (RRAG). The establishment of the RRAG was a milestone in the development of race-relations policy. Its terms of reference were fairly wide. Moreover, it had no executive or financial powers and was served by only one officer.

Community Consultations

Soon after the inception of RRAG the Council held a reception in the City Hall for leaders of most ethnic minority organisations in the city. Following this reception the RRAG held direct consultations with some of these organisation and summarised its findings in the document called *The Other Man's Views,* released in April 1982. A major concern of South Asian parents emerged as Westernisation and Christianisation of their children through education. Muslim organisations, particularly the Muslim Parents' Association and the Bradford Council for Mosques articulated their concerns with ferocity previously unknown to local councillors and council officers. Racial attacks in and around schools and the treatment of adolescent girls in schools were further major concerns. Anxieties were also expressed about adequate access to housing grants, and the refusal of planning permission for certain type of changes to inner-city houses, the establishment of mosques and *madrasas* (religious education and mother-tongue schools) and Asian food takeaways etc.

Parallel to *The Other Man's View* a working party of four women councillors presented the findings of their consultation sessions with ethnic minority women in its report *A Chance To Speak.* These consultations added an additional perspective on the areas covered by *The Other Man's View* sometimes supporting its findings and in places offering a directly contradictory viewpoint. For example, whilst men were seeking financial support for and an expansion of supplementary language schools, Asian women had a number of strong practical concerns about them and suggested that the provision for the teaching of mother-tongues and religious education should be within the main school curriculum. Additionally, they raised concerns about the adequacy and appropriateness of health services and of separate, 'women only', recreational facilities and centres for social activities, English tuition classes, girls-only schools and youth provision for girls.

Almost all those consulted expressed an urgent need for the establishment of community centres for minority ethnic communities and to redress the particular needs of young and elderly people in the minority communities. The West Indian groups were particularly concerned that many council services for ethnic minorities only acknowledged the Asian community and ignored the needs of West Indians, a concern that continues even today.

Consequences of Community Consultations

They led to a rapid growth in the number of ethnic minority organisations. They enhanced the confidence of minority communities to raise their specific concerns about the way Council policies affected them and encouraged them to make demands to meet their normal needs more effectively and for their special needs to be considered more favourably.

The Council took a number of initiatives, for instance to meet the needs of elderly, Muslim women and to accommodate the special cultural and religious needs of ethnic minority children in schools in a very short period of time.

The Council realised that there was an urgent need for 'self-development' and the need to create self-help organisations within the ethnic minority communities. The Council used its community programme grant received from Central Government under the "Urban Programme" towards this purpose fairly effectively. Through these grants many of the ethnic minority groups built up equivalent social and cultural facilities to those enjoyed by other sections of the population. On the positive side the minority communities were able to create facilities to meet their own prioritised needs and according to their own customs. However, encouraged by the availability of local funds, a number of fake and inefficient organisations sprang up with little grassroots support. The whole process of decision-making about grant allocation became highly politicised. To some extent it increased the already existing divisiveness within and between minority community groups in the city. However the long-term broad impact of this initiative certainly out-weighted its immediate weaknesses.

Common Themes of the 1980s Approach

Bradford Council's approach to race relations in the 1980s maintained some basic features over the period.

All political parties generally supported the overall race relations policy. The implementation of the policy, however, did create diverse political reactions. For example, Eric Pickles, the Conservative Party Leader, declared that he and his party were fully committed to race relations work but would like to shift the earlier emphasis from employment to "service delivery". However, the Labour leadership saw "recruitment and selection in employment" as the priority areas of concern. The initial major emphasis on recruitment and selection in employment was maintained.

Action on the employment front remained the prime goal of the Council. For instance, the Management Committee in its document (approved on 16 February 1982) declared that

> "The Council is determined to be an equal opportunities employer and to reflect in a detailed and practical way that Bradford is and will remain a multi-cultural community....We now require of all our managers that they take effective action to correct racial disadvantage. We will expect this to be seen evidenced by the figures of the number of people from the ethnic minorities applying and being appointed to the Council's service changing significantly in the immediate future. If this does not occur, all those responsible will be held to account for their actions to the elected Members and to the senior management of the Council as appropriate."

With regard to the "effective action" the document made it clear that it was "remedial action" and not "positive discrimination" that was intended.

The Council did not establish any special race relations unit at the centre to oversee the implementation or monitoring of its policy. Individual directorates and committees remained responsible for establishing race-relations policies in their own respective areas. During its lifetime all policies were received and approved by RRAG to achieve consistency. Policies in different areas of Council activities were developed, implemented, monitored and evaluated for their effectiveness. Despite the obvious advantages of this approach in terms of 'local relevance, ownership and responsibility' in a large organisation like the Council the speed and extent of progress varied considerably in different directorates. Thus the overall success of the Council's policy remained patchy.

The training of key council staff in race related issues and cultural awareness was a major plank of the new policy. A number of race trainers were appointed in various directorates to facilitate the implementation of their policies. For many officers attendance at the cultural awareness and racism awareness training courses proved a painful experience. Despite some serious resistance to the compulsory requirement of this training, most officers and elected member attended these courses. On the whole race trainers had a powerful influence on staff training.

Little punishment was considered or accorded to those who resented, criticised or even refused to accept the broad thrust of the race training courses and the policy in general. The overall approach was to "promote, cajole and encourage" officers to implement the "Race Relations Plans". (2)

Main Achievement of Race Relations Policy
The major outcome of the high profile race relations policy was the empowerment of ethnic minority communities. The Council became more accessible to these communities and the communities realised that they had a role in shaping and influencing the Council's policies.

The whole process opened up new channels of communication between public sector organisations and ethnic minority groups. These links proved enormously helpful in maintaining harmonious relations and easing tensions in highly explosive situations such as the 'Gulf War Crisis' and the 'Satanic Verses Affair' in the early 1990s.

Race became an additional, recognised dimension in the development of new policies for the Council.

Education provision and the school curriculum were most critically affected by the new policy. A number of positive changes were made in schools provision to accommodate the particular views and concerns of the local Muslim community.

'Positive Action' initiatives, particularly to increase the employment opportunities for ethnic minority young people in areas such as social work and council offices quite rapidly increased their numbers in some directorates. However their concentration in lower level jobs with limited opportunities for promotion did result in industrial tribunal cases. The proportion of black staff in the Council increased from 1.8% in 1982 to 4.6% in 1987.

Consequences of a High Profile Approach

A high profile approach required a political consensus and active co-operation between all major political parties and their members in the Council. However, such commitment proved difficult to sustain over a long period. It resulted in individual casualties in local elections. For example, Peter Gilmour, a Conservative candidate, lost his seat in Keighley North for his outright support for the provision of *Halal* meat in schools for Muslim children. Political opportunism at party or individual level became tempting but resulted in harmful consequences to the overall cause. The campaign to oust Honeyford demonstrated such opportunism quite clearly.

A high profile thrust on a massive programme of racism awareness training resulted in a good deal of disquiet and resentment in City Hall. This became one of the main issues in the Honeyford Affair that sent tremors through the city's otherwise mainly peaceful political environment. Bradford's high profile initiatives not only attracted media attention but also the attention of racist political parties with a wish to enhance their membership and to seek publicity for their views.

The gap between policy and practice caused more problems through unmet raised expectations. The officers of the Council came under enormous pressure both from the elected members and the leadership of ethnic minority organisations. The high profile policy did result in a series of racial discrimination cases in employment and promotion against the Council.

'Normalisation' or making the 'race-relations' dimension an integral natural dimension in policy developments was taking much longer than expected. Raised expectations when not fully met caused more problems than they resolved. The high number of race discrimination related industrial tribunal cases against the Council overshadowed the gains the minority communities made in their substantially increased numbers in the local authority's employment.

Ethnic politics around various activities of the Council such as the distribution of financial resources through community grants became highly significant and resulted in fault lines developing within and between ethnic minority communities. These divisions could only serve to limit the impact which the various communities could make upon mainstream institutions.

With race as a central dimension in policy making (implicitly or explicitly) the 'class' and 'gender' dimensions appeared somewhat ignored. However, in the case of ethnic minority communities, not to deal with these other dimensions as well, is to seriously undermine the reduction that can be achieved in the overall levels of disadvantage.

Adoption of an equal opportunities policy presented some conceptual and practical difficulties to the policy makers. For example, three concepts in equal opportunities caused major difficulties and attracted wide-spread criticism.
(a) Positive action was normally confused with positive discrimination, which means discrimination in reverse or in favour of ethnic minorities. This is illegal in Britain.

(b) Ethnic target setting to achieve fair representation of ethnic minorities in certain fields, for example, in employment, housing and so on were deliberately confused with the setting of quotas, which is illegal. Not only that, quotas are criticised by both whites and ethnic minorities, although for different reasons. Whites resent quotas as 'unnecessary favouritism' whilst black and Asians resent them because of the 'stigma' which they make it possible to attach to employment success. Targets are intended to relate to 'fair representation'. However what constitutes fair representation is problematic. The common advice that fair representation means a figure equivalent to the proportion of the minority population locally or nationally, as a guide is not a satisfactory answer in every situation. Such a figure ignores minority groups' particular preferences or choices, and may thus remain unrealistic and difficult to achieve in practice.

(c) Ethnic monitoring is argued to be an absolute necessity for measuring the results of equal opportunity policies and for establishing the levels of race / ethnic inequalities. It presents some real difficulties in relation to satisfactory classification and the cost of collecting and analysing the statistics. Critics of collecting ethnic data argued that highlighting ethnicity creates unnecessary dangers of data misuse by setting 'minimum targets' (only to protect public or legal criticism) and of the information falling into the wrong hands. This argument has now lost weight in Britain. However, there was little evidence that the Council was using this tool effectively for its intended objectives.

Racism Awareness Training

Racism Awareness Training (RAT) that was made obligatory for all council officers involved in the recruitment of staff created a climate of hostility. Tensions between the trainers and the delegates to the training workshops were always strong. Black trainers were openly complaining about the inadequacy of support they needed to confront many of the delegates' resentment of the suggestion that racism was a 'white peoples' problem, thus, implying that they were all 'individually racists' and all white institutions suffered from 'institutional racism'. Black trainers at times suffered out and out abuse from white delegates. On the other hand, white trainers have had to learn to become more openly 'anti-racist' themselves. This led to the training packages being revised too often and to their being turned into 'cultural awareness' courses. A cynical assessment of the racism awareness and cultural awareness courses by some critics suggested that they were making the practitioners more careful and sophisticated in discrimination. It appeared as if 'direct discrimination' was turning into 'indirect discrimination'. One thing was sure, that such courses were not easy to run as white people had so much to unlearn before they could begin to understand and appreciate what 'racism' meant in practice and its consequences for the 'non-whites'.

The critics of 'equal opportunities' frequently quote the American race relations expert, Thomas Sowell. He believes that race relations experts advocate the achievement of success in life not through hard work, self-discipline and a sense of purpose, but through the insidious paraphernalia of historic disadvantage, reverse discrimination and ultimately, quota systems. A recipe for a race relations disaster. Such a criticism of the British race advisers is an extreme exaggeration of their approach and a total misrepresentation of the anti discrimination legislation and its supporters. (3)

The Policy Unit Report

The Policy Unit of the Council carried out a review of the three years working of race relations policy in the mid1980s. Its report, *Race Relations in Bradford: the Council's Approach* admitted, firstly, that the Council had been too vulnerable to criticism of its policies because it had not clearly explained their necessity to the people of Bradford and its employees. Secondly, it had failed to deflate the myths and stereotypes, in fact, may have encouraged some of them. A major weakness that the report stressed was the Council's focus on 'problems' rather than the focus being on 'the potential strengths of a multi-racial society'. The review also recognised the lack of sophistication in the policy monitoring and evaluation systems. It also identified that "institutional racism" was not fully understood and readily admitted by most employees, the issue of racial harassment was inadequately addressed and some areas of the Council remained untouched so far.

The struggle for racial justice

Race Becomes a Part of Equal Rights

In the early 1980s, council officers and elected members put enormous efforts into making the race relations policy work. It is depressing to note that the pace at which some considerable progress was made in the early 1980s lost all momentum towards the end of 1980s. Then inertia and complacency set in. The Council had lost five Industrial Tribunal cases where racial discrimination was found against it and in three of these cases exemplary damages were awarded. Another 30/40 cases were already in the pipeline. The number of such cases was building up year by year. This built up the public perception, particularly amongst the ethnic minority population, that Bradford was a 'racist council'.

Towards the end of the 1980s the race relations policy went into limbo for a number of years. For example, no analysis was undertaken of the ethnic composition of the Council employees in 1986 and in the years 1988 through 1991.

It was not until October 1991 that the Council issued it's *Equal Rights Statement* document. (see Appendix B) In line with the national trend the Council decided to deal with race equality issues within its general 'equal rights' approach. Thus, in the 1990s it had no separate race relations policy. At present race issues are considered and dealt with under the *"Equal Rights Statement"* issued in October 1991.

The Council was now extremely worried. Its Chief Executive, Richard Penn, with the consent of politicians commissioned (in October 1992) John Carr, an external consultant, to fully investigate the state of race relations in the Council and make recommendations to redress the situation.

Carr's report, *Alibis for Inaction: A report on aspects of the City of Bradford Metropolitan Council's procedures for handling complaints of discrimination,* produced startling findings. John Carr said that

> *"the council's equal opportunities policy appeared to be out of control and flying in the face of its commitment to good race relations".*

122

The story of Bradford 1950-2002

He made two major points: (a) that there were no Council-wide comprehensive 'management systems' in place to implement and monitor race relations policies and the reported cases of discrimination, and (b) that nothing happened to those caught breaking the equal opportunity policy. The Telegraph & Argus (9 March 1993) made the report a front-page headline *"RACE RAP SHOCK AT CITY HALL"*. Responding to the report's findings, the Labour Leader of the Council, Gerry Sutcliffe said, "he was determined to eradicate any hint of discrimination". The Council accepted all 25 recommendations of the report for immediate action.

What was happening in Bradford wasn't unique to Bradford but what went to the credit of Bradford Council was its courage to publish the report for public consumption. John Carr told the Bradford Racial Equality Council meeting on 22 June 1993 that his report was a genuine and honest reporting of the situation as at no stage either politicians or officers put any pressure on him to water down the expression of the problems and his recommendations. He believed that because of the fast increasing cynicism about the Council's commitment, belief in its policies and its failure to get positive results from them the Council wanted the issues raised and the procedural weaknesses exposed and dealt with.

In July 1991 the CRE under considerable pressure from the local Race Equality Council threatened to take proceedings against the Council under Section 62 of the RRA 1976 for persistent discrimination. Such proceedings were actually served on the Council in October 1991. However, in 1995 the CRE agreed to postpone its proceedings after reaching an agreement with the Council. The Council gave eight undertakings including ones to take appropriate disciplinary action as a result of findings of unlawful racial discrimination by the Industrial Tribunal or County Court and to implement the recommendations of the Carr Report *"Alibis for Inaction"*.

It appeared that the Council was brought on track once again to examine its commitment and procedures to make progress in eliminating racial discrimination and inequalities in its provision of services. The Council worked to build 'Equal Rights Issues' into its overall Services Planning

Process. Services Strategic Plans for different directorates were regularly prepared. It adopted the CRE guide *Racial Equality Means Quality: Standard for Racial Equality for Local Government in England and Wales* in July 1995 to regularly assess and monitor its progress in all directorates. Codes of practice and procedures in employment were reviewed. The Council in implementing the recommendations of the Carr Report made a good deal of progress. By the end of 1998 the CRE expressed its satisfaction about the implementation of the 1995 agreement between the Commission and the Council.

Again another contributory factor to the Council's action was the Manningham race disturbances in the summer of 1995. These street disturbances gave a further reminder to the Council about the lack of any effective policy measures to improve race relations in the city and to deal with the serious situation of race inequalities in employment, education and housing. The Council published its response to the Bradford Congress Reports on these riots on 25 March 1997. The Council's document *Response to the Bradford Commission Reports* was 43 pages long. The document was full of explanations of the Council strategies, action plans with very clearly marked implementation and achievement dates. The Council displayed a clear understanding that its responses would be judged by the results achieved.

> *"The Council fully accepts that in the event, it will be judged by what it does, not by what it says, which is why this report has avoided vision statements and gone for concrete proposals, with targets and time-scales." (p. 43)*

However, it qualified its commitment by providing no firm guarantee for the full implementation of the proposals.

> *"We believe the proposals are challenging and innovative. It should be recognised however that achievement will be difficult in the present national political and economic climate and with current restrictions on budgets. The proposals are put forward as the basis for consultation, and we will continue to consult*

and learn from the best practice of others as we translate the plans and targets into action." (p. 3)

Given this lack of firm commitment, it will not be surprising that the action plans have remained uncompleted or totally abandoned.

The Council produced its first Community Plan in 1996 and in it race issues became an integral part of the overall strategy for the Council's activities and priorities for the inner city areas. Race was disguised under 'cultural diversity' or 'equal opportunity' or 'equal rights' phrases. Under its Community Consultation & Participation Strategy, the Council started consulting and involving communities in its community development plans. For example, in 1999-2000 it used its 80 Neighbourhood Forums, the "Speak-Out" Citizen's Panel and direct reply-paid mail-shots as part of the consultation processes. However, the biggest and the most high profile consultation event was, *"2020 Vision"*, seeking the views of all Bradford's citizens to make the District "a great place to live, learn, work and play".

According to the Council's document: *Making a Difference: Best Value Performance Plan 2000-2001*,

> *" the vision is primarily a vision of the District's economy, as this will shape every other aspect of life in 2020, but it also includes social and environmental issues which will need to be tackled if the vision is to be achieved."*

Among the ten main features of the *2020 Vision* two particular ones, that directly relate to the achievement of racial justice and equality of opportunity, are:

> *"A new sense of identity, developed out of the positive inter-action between the District's different cultures.*
> *An **inclusive** District, with equal rights and equal opportunities for all, and which has reversed the inner-outer polarisation of the late 20th century".*

It is too early to comment on how these priorities are to be achieved or being currently acted upon. Part of the answers may emerge from the implementation of the recommendations made by the Lord Ouseley Report (released in July 2001) about the present state of race relations and the future of racial equality in the District. This report (as described in detail in chapter15) presents the findings of the Bradford Race Review Panel set up in November 2000 after two consultation meetings of a group of people representing a wide range of interests. A number of key local organisations including the Bradford Council are currently preparing their responses to the Ouseley Report. The responsibility for co-ordinating and monitoring their action plans has been assigned to the Bradford Vision, a reconstituted form of Bradford Congress. No such plans have been made public for information or debate as yet (May 2002).

13

MULTICULTURAL EDUCATION: AN EXPERIMENT IN GOOD RACE RELATIONS

Immigrant Education: 1960s-1970s

Up to the middle of the 1960s Bradford had no specific policy on the education of immigrant children. The number of children arriving from overseas was small and they were easily accommodated by the spare capacity in most schools in the inner-city area where their parents had settled. With the sudden increase in the numbers arriving in 1964 Bradford Education Committee decided on *certain practical solutions* to the known problems (as the Committee put it). The Committee decided three points of general policy (a) No school was to have more than 25 per cent of immigrant children on the roll. This became the basis for the 'policy of dispersal'. (b) Up to nine years of age, non-English speaking children were to be taught in normal classes to take advantage of the 'rubbing-off' effect. Older children were to be taught in special classes. (c) All immigrant children were to be thoroughly medically tested before starting school for worms, tuberculosis etc. (1)

This policy was implemented until the Local Government Reorganisation of 1974. The Educational Services Committee of the reorganised Bradford Council set up a working party, including elected Council members, education officers and teachers, to review the current policies on the education of immigrants. The author was co-opted to this Joint Working Party in his capacity of Chairman of the Education Panel of Bradford Community Relations Council. The Working Party examined in depth the educational, social and general reasons for the continuation of the dispersal policy and the potential consequences of abandoning it. On balance, after considering some changes in its implementation arrangements, its recommendation to the Education Services Committee in the report: *Education in a Multi-Racial City: The Report of the Joint Working Party on the Education of Immigrants and their Children, August, 1976* was that the policy be continued

The author's view was that the dispersal policy, despite the real hardships it created for children and parents, was the only way at the time to minimise the educational disadvantage of immigrant children. The only alternative to bussing for achieving the full benefit from the educational system was for the immigrant population to disperse more widely in the district. However, some local immigrant leaders were opposed to the policy of bussing of children and did not see the spatial dispersal of immigrant families possible in the 1970s. Despite the practical difficulties that bussing of children was causing to the parents many of them were ready to accept the inconveniences it was creating. In terms of the pure political ideology of race relations in the 1970s, the policy could be argued as racially discriminatory, as only black and Asian children were bussed to maintain a racial balance in local schools. This was the main ground on which it was ultimately declared to be discriminatory and finally phased out in Bradford.

Multicultural Education in the 1980s

Alongside the employment front, education became the major service area to be reviewed under the 1981 race relations policy statement. The public policy objective on the immigrant children's education was:

> "To ensure that the children of immigrant parents, as in the case of all children, receive the education best suited to their ages, abilities and aptitudes. The LEA was devoting considerable resources under Section 11 funding to achieve this objective". (2)

Included amongst the major policy development initiatives in two new Local Administrative Memorandums (LAMs) were the provision of halal meat for Muslim children in schools, steps to develop a multi-cultural curriculum and changes in the provision of religious education and morning school assemblies.

The first LAM was issued to all schools in November 1982. It reminded schools of the Council's race relations policy statement *"that Bradford has both a multi-racial and multi-cultural population and that all sections of the community have an equal right to the maintenance of their distinctive identities and loyalties of culture, language, religion and custom."*

It stressed "ways in which schools and teachers should be sensitive to individual needs in a community of mixed races". The LAM contained practical advice to schools on matters such as the parental right to withdraw children from religious education, religious assemblies and to celebrate their own religious festivals. Schools were asked to provide room for Muslim prayers where requested and to allow Muslim children to leave school early to attend Friday prayers. Parents' wishes were acknowledged with regard to the wearing of school uniform, certain items of religious identity (such as the Sikh *Kara* or Muslim Tawiz), participation in mixed physical education lessons, the contents of school-meals, and the recording of Asian names. In all these areas Asian parents had expressed serious concerns that the established practices and expectations of teachers were ignoring Asian children and their parents' own cultural and religious traditions and requirements.

The second LAM issued a year later in November 1983 dealt with racialist behaviour in schools. It explained to teachers what constituted racialist behaviour, gave advice on identifying and dealing with racial incidents and required schools to maintain records of such incidents and regularly report to the appropriate Assistant Director of Education.

These directives addressed some of the practical concerns of ethnic minority parents, formally reaffirmed the practices already being followed by some schools, but at the same time, met resistance and resentment from the heads of those schools where the numbers of Asian children were small. Whilst agreeing that most of the requirements were 'good educational practices', their imposition as 'formal requirements' was considered a diminution of head teachers' discretion and authority and, therefore, an unnecessary interference. For the Council, non-observance of these directives would be a challenge to their right to determine policy and practices.

The struggle for racial justice

1,570 say no to bussing

The petition, organised by the Indian Workers' Association, was signed by 1,570 people.
It was received by Coun. Mrs. Dorothy Moore, chairman of the Special Services Panel, and Mr. Philip Bendall, chief special services officer.
Coun. Moore said the petition would certainly be referred to the council's immigrant review body, consisting of councillors and officers.

A large delegation yesterday presented a petition against Bradford Metropolitan Council's policy of bussing Asian children to schools some miles from their homes.

Mr. Mohammed Ajeeb, chairman of the Metropolitan Community Relations Council, was present when the petition was handed in, along with representatives of the Indian Workers' Association, Sikh temples, the Southfield

Square mosque, other Asian organisations and the Campaign against Racism and Fascism in Bradford. Members of the Asian Youth Movement were present.

● Picture shows Mr. Ajeeb handing the petition to Coun. Moore.

Telegraph & Argus 6 March 1979

Abolition of the Bussing Policy

Bradford LEA's policies of dispersing immigrant children through 'bussing' across the city and the progression of all newly arriving ethnic minority children through Junior and Senior Language Centres in the city had attracted a great deal of opposition from the Muslim Parents' Association from the early1970s. The local CRC's impact on local educational policies remained fairly weak until it was given a place on the Advisory Committee for the Education of Immigrant Children in 1974. In May 1977 the Indian Workers' Association presented a petition signed by 1500 people to the LEA for the abolition of bussing arrangements. Eventually, after an investigation by the Commission for Racial Equality which declared the bussing policy racially discriminatory, it was phased out from September 1980.

By this time the debate about the concept of 'multicultural education' had gained ground. A serious challenge was mounted to the 1960s school curriculum perspective of promoting only British traditions, history, customs, and culture and the teaching of *Standard* English. . The *'colour and culture blind'* assimilation model changed in some respects in the 1970s to accommodate the demands of black and Asian parents' strong declared preferences for the retention of their cultural and religious identities, and their community languages. Many schools started valuing the positive aspects of the bilingualism of Asian children and encouraged it. New topics concerning black and South Asian religions, cultures, history and the geography of areas of immigrant origin were gradually, albeit superficially, introduced. The celebration of Asian festivals in primary schools gained popularity and *'saris, samosas and steel bands'* became an integral part of such celebrations. This *'soft multi-cultural education'* caught the imagination of most teachers. However, it did not have much impact on the basic racist attitudes of many teachers. Institutional racism in education was hardly challenged and most importantly the nature and extent of 'racial disadvantage' for ethnic minority children remained unchanged.

In the beginning of the 1980s the *'Multicultural Education Perspective'* took a new turn. With the Council's adoption of race relations policy, the LEA signed up to *'the Equality Perspective'* in education. It defined the aims of education in Bradford as:

1. *To seek ways of preparing all children and young people in a multi-cultural society.*
2. *To counter racism and racist attitudes, and the inequalities and discrimination which results from them.*
3. *To build on and develop the strengths of cultural and linguistic diversity.*
4. *To respond sensitively to the special needs of minority groups.*

In pursuit of these aims the Directorate of Educational Services published its document *Towards Education For All* containing basic principles, advice and guidelines for changes in a number of school curriculum areas. The Council also introduced changes in religious education through its *The Agreed Syllabus 1983: Religious Education for Living in Today's World* that enshrined the aim of developing an understanding of and respect for minority religions in the city. Supplementary schools providing religious education and the teaching of community languages were supported.

In 1983 the Muslim Parents' Association (MPA) submitted an application to take over six local schools. Their application attracted immediate opposition and the public reaction occupied enormous space in the T & A for months on end. It also received a very strong negative reaction from Muslim parents and the leaders of Bradford Council for Mosques, the bid being labelled the 'one-man bandwagon' of Mr Riaz Shahid who had contested local elections against other Muslim candidates in 1973 and 1979, albeit unsuccessfully. The Asian Youth Movement's Chairman, J Rashid, was particularly critical of the demand for Muslim schools fearing it would only serve to increase racist tendencies in the city.

Up to the middle of the 1980s, despite the presence of some practical difficulties in the implementation of these radical changes in the education of ethnic minority children, it appeared that the new direction in 'multi-cultural education' was largely acceptable to schools. The notion of multi-cultural education was appealing even to the reluctant liberal section of the population as it realised that in a place like Bradford, unless the educational system developed children's understanding of *all cultures* present in the city, peaceful co-existence in the future would remain extremely fragile. To the LEA and the moderate Muslims in Bradford changes introduced through the multi-cultural policy averted threats from organisations such as the MPA to make further attempts to take over some state schools and convert them into Islamic schools. Many perceived the advent of official multi-cultural policies in Council services as a natural check on the spread of Islamic fundamentalism from a negligible minority to the younger generation in any substantial numbers. It was seen as extremely important in preserving race relation's delicate equilibrium.

Nationally, the discussions about an appropriate educational approach to multi-racial, multi-cultural, multi-faith and multi-lingual Britain moved from 'multi-culturism' to 'anti-racism'. In Bradford the debate between 'multi-cultural education' and 'anti-racist education' remained as confused as it was at the national level. There was little common understanding of 'racism', 'racialism' and 'anti-racist' terms. In Bradford, despite a strong lobby for 'anti-racist' education a cool response from many head teachers limited change to the minimum required of them by the authority's policy statement on race relations.

However, the *Halal* meat debate and the *Honeyford affair* brought to the surface the so far repressed opposition to the measures introduced through the policy and practices of multi-cultural education in city schools. In 1993, Bangladeshi parents took the LEA to the High Court challenging its policy on allocation of secondary school places. They were unsuccessful in proving that the policy was racially discriminatory. However, two significant aspects of their action were: that they were prepared to use the 'parent power' tool to challenge an authority, and that the abolition of the 'bussing policy' had resulted in their exclusion from some of the best schools.

During the 1990s there were no serious discussions on the nature of the multicultural policy that Bradford had or ought to have. The implementation of the National Curriculum and other national initiatives in education have been the main concerns of the LEA. The current practice in multicultural education in the city is graphically illustrated in the latest (2000) publication of the Bradford Education Services, *Cultural Diversity in Practice: A Good Practice Guide For Schools*.

The recent Ofsted Report: *Inspection Of Bradford Local Education Authority, May 2000* is a testimony of failure. The report is critical of the current situation on a number of points. *Firstly*, that the targets that had been set, under the Government's Ethnic Minority Targets for Achievement Grant (EMTAG), for attainment by Pakistani and Bangladeshi children were too low. *Secondly*, the Authority has been criticised for failure to collect statistics in a systematic manner and for consequently not being able to make appropriate use of them in order to address some longstanding problems. *Thirdly*, the resources available for supporting minority ethnic pupils were not being devoted on the basis of 'actual pupils' needs'. Concern was also raised about the competence of some former Section 11 Staff in relation to their new role within the EMTAG scheme. *Fourthly*, that the LEA was providing limited amount of support for pupils returning from extended leave abroad. At the same time it was evident that discussions with local communities had not entirely tackled the implications of extended leave abroad either. (3)

Bradford has always boasted of its good practices in the education of minority ethnic community children. In some ways it seems to be a false claim. The success of the multicultural education policy and practice in the city can be evaluated from different standpoints. One of the objectives that the multicultural approach in schools will make education more appropriate and relevant to children from minority ethnic communities appears to have been achieved at least in one respect, that is, in making the broad educational experience and environment in schools multicultural. However, its impact on the level of educational achievement of children from minority ethnic communities is uncertain. Some minority groups, Indians for example, are showing demonstrably higher gains than the major group of Pakistani children whose low achievement levels is a major concern.

It was also expected that multicultural education would develop and promote good inter-community relations through learning about diverse cultures, religions, historical relationships, and thus in turn enhance mutual understanding and respect within the ethnically diverse school population. Almost three decades later, racial harassment in schools and outside of them is still a major issue. Respect for diversity of cultures is only at the 'tolerance level'. Racial disturbances on the city streets are frequent. Polarisation of white and minority ethnic communities is abundantly visible. Suspicion and mistrust between white and minority communities on the one hand, and within the different minority communities themselves on the other, have failed to lessen tensions within the social and political environment. In the absence of any formal research-based evidence the contemporary model of local multicultural education policy and practice presents all the signs of a less than successful experience or experiment.

14

2001: A YEAR OF RIOTS

Bradford captured the media headlines the world over during the seven-day period of 8 July to 14 July. Two major events—the four consecutive nights of riots on its streets followed by the publication of a major Race Review report by Lord Herman Ouseley on the state of race relations in the city - happened by coincidence rather than by design. Covering the weekend events of 'burning Bradford', the Telegraph & Argus published a seventeen page 'Riots Special' edition on Monday, 9 July, with the front page heading, WHERE DO WE GO FROM HERE. It contained graphic details of the incidents and the pictures of horrific destruction on the streets.

Earlier that Easter (15 April 2001) over one hundred Asian gang members clashed with white youths for more than six hours in the Lidget Green and Great Horton areas of Bradford. Trouble started at the Coach House Pub when some white youths (believed to be skinheads) made racist jibes at the guests attending a private Asian (Hindu) celebration. Very quickly the trouble spread to the street and during the rampage pubs and shops were smashed, 17 cars were burnt in one garage alone and a number of people were seriously hurt. A large contingent of police in riot gear was involved in controlling the mayhem and restoring peace. Police made some 100 arrests. The violence sent a shock wave around local communities.

After what happened in Oldham (in May) and Burnley (in June) something bigger, more damaging and explosive was expected to happen in Bradford. And so it did. For four consecutive nights Bradford witnessed violence on the streets, the worst violence since the Manningham riots of 1995. It was sparked off as a reaction to rumours that a large number of BNP supporters were coming to the city in the wake of a ban imposed on their proposed demonstration in the city.

The struggle for racial justice

Some blamed the eruption of violence on the decision by its organisers to cancel the Bradford Festival finale on Saturday, 7 July 2001. This decision was taken on the advice of police and Council leaders in view of a threat of violence from NF/ BNP supporters and the determination of the Anti-Nazi League to counter the NF's offensive. A peaceful rally of 500-700 Anti-Nazi League supporters heard that an Asian youth was beaten up by skinheads drinking in a pub in Ivegate a short distance away from Centenary Square in the city centre. Within minutes the disrupted rally of largely Asian Muslim youth became an angry mob and the entire city centre turned into a battlefield between a large contingent of police and hundreds of youths. The riot police lines were pelted with bricks, glass bottles, fireworks and petrol bombs. Running battles between the youths and the police continued well into the early hours and quickly spread over a large area of Asian concentration in the White Abbey Road, Manningham, Carlisle Road and Whetley Hill areas.

Fires gutted dozens of cars, a garage full of BMW cars, three pubs, two clubs, an Asian restaurant and a number of other properties in one night. Sporadic outbreaks of violence continued on the following Sunday. On Saturday, almost 1000 police officers were involved in patrolling the streets of Bradford. More than 260 officers were injured in the operation and by Monday some 60 people had been arrested and charged. The damage caused during the riots is estimated to be well over £25 million. The policing bill for the riots soared by £250,000 a day.

Fire gutted BMW garage.
Photograph by kind permission of Tim Smith

During Monday and Tuesday nights the disturbances spread to white estates. Mobs of white youths rioted and clashed with police. Disturbances on the streets of Holmewood, Ravenscliffe, Fagley and Bierley estates further away from the city centre were described as 'revenge' or 'tit for tat' race attacks. Three Asian-owned restaurants were damaged and the police made 24 arrests. For the police it was an unexpected and new situation to tackle.

Among the ruins of the bridges between the sharply divided, religiously polarised and spatially segregated communities of Bradford, some fairly *standard* explanations were offered for the causes of violence. The range of explanations for the riots varied tremendously.

Jim Greenhalf (T&A, 17 July 2001) quotes Ian Vine from Bradford University: "The primary underlying factor in the readiness to riot is not white racism or police incompetence; nor material deprivation. Rather, it is the motivation of an alienated minority of Muslim youth to assert power in the one way they know -coercive 'control of the street' in primarily Asian local neighbourhoods." For the root cause of their alienation Vine refers to the exclusion of these youth from "the decision-making about the future of their own ethnic religious community here" by its "supposed leaders" who encourage "ethnic self-segregation" and inhibit the propagation of "liberal values" for their "self-aggrandisement". Mathew Parris (The Times, 14 July 2001) argued that the "outbreaks of violence are explained by the human appetite for violence. Breaking things is fun. Torching a leisure centre is itself a leisure activity. A fight between an Asian gang and a BNP gang satisfies the same instincts as tennis." Following such a theory, the current riots can be explained as 'riots to satisfy a desire for rioting'. This does make some sense when you see boys (no girls) as young as 12-16 years of age involved in the violent clashes with the police.

The spate of rioting by youths, white on the estates and Muslim in the Manningham area, within their own territorial boundaries, is a clear indication of the presence of some common factors. These factors may include social deprivation, unemployment, disaffection of some youths from their own communities, and the hatred of police authority. Many believed it was the reaction of these disaffected youths to such deep rooted social problems of poverty, low educational achievement, poor physical environment, and in the case of Muslim youths, the additional impact of institutional racism, racial / religious discrimination from which their families suffer. However, left-wing politics and the presence of right-wing extremists racialise these social ills that otherwise affect sections of the white and the non-white populations in equal proportions. Whilst others claimed these factors to be irrelevant "excuses", especially in the context of the present events in Bradford.

Words such as *mindless, senseless, criminality and thuggery* were splashed all over the newspapers to describe the events in Bradford. The destruction had been mindless and done by a small group of hard core criminals and thugs. Some put it down to the provocation caused by the extreme Right parties such as the National Front and the BNP.

The lack of consultation with community groups in the decision to cancel the Bradford Festival finale is believed to be a significant factor in the incident. It is argued that cancelling the programme purely on the threat of the NF was a moral victory for the NF. It played into the NF strategy to destroy the peace of the city. Then Muslim youths did their work for them.

Alongside a tremendous general level of support for the police handling of the riots there was a good deal of criticism too. Asians complain that the police neglected their security; reacted too slowly to their problems and incidents of racial attacks and harassment; had an overpowering presence at the political rally; were indiscriminately heavy-handed in dealing with the crowd and so on. The police were blamed for not acting swiftly and firmly with a small number of white known Nazis in the mob and for being harsh with young Asians. Whites accuse the police of being too lenient with Asian thugs, criminals and other lawbreakers, to the extent of being scared of touching them. For the police it is a no win situation, either they are accused of doing too little and too late, or they are blamed for over reaction.

In its Comment column the Telegraph & Argus (9 July 2001) repeated the statement it made after the Bradford Commission report into the Manningham riots of 1995.

The story of Bradford 1950-2002

"In Bradford there is racial hatred; there is fear; there is ignorance; there is dire unemployment; there is poverty and deprivation; there is religious fundamentalism; there is political extremism; there is petty politics; there is ineptitude and incompetence; there is misplaced optimism and apathy; there are good intentions, and there are evil ones."

Have any of the features in the life of Bradford identified above changed in any significant way since the publication of the Bradford Commission report almost five years ago? The simple answer is *NO*. Even a superficial analysis of recent events suggests that a small minority of white Bradfordians harbour deep-seated racial hatred and resentment of police authority. Likewise, a tiny minority of fundamentalist Muslim youths hate the police, the local authority and have contempt for western culture and life styles. Like their white counterparts they detest the liberal secular features of Bradford's multicultural reality. This minority also includes some hardcore drug-pushers and criminal thugs who were involved in the violent clashes. It was evident that the majority of so-called "alienated Muslim youth" were not implicated in the riots.

It is widely recognised that these riots seriously dented the general image of the city and would have dire consequences for inward future investment into the local economy as well as for the slowly developing tourist industry in the District. Furthermore, the 'self-segregation' of the Muslim community is likely to deepen. Therefore, the recommendations of a recent report on housing in the city, *Breaking Down the Barriers* (1) for improving Asian access to social rented housing outside the *South Asian ghettoes* in the city will remain unachieved given the heightened insecurity caused by the riots.

The present riots in Bradford have been compared with the disturbances in Belfast which occurred during the Orange Marches. Simon Jenkin (The Times, 11 July 2001) wrote:

"Bradford, like Belfast, has communities polarised by religion, migration and history. In both cities trouble began with complaints of discrimination. In both a failure of political reform left fertile ground for vigilantes and agitators. Belfast

139

The struggle for racial justice

ended in partition. Bradford is said to be going the same way. There is even talk of "peace walls" on the British mainland".

The suggestions for the use of water cannons, batons and plastic bullets to deal with the rioters brought the Bradford situation much more close to that in Belfast. The recent shipment of some bulletproof vehicles from Belfast for future use in Bradford is turning it into a reality.

It is also suggested that *"no-go'* Asian as well as white areas exist in Bradford as these do in Oldham and Burnley. As there are no boundary walls that mark the beginnings and ends of individual communities, that is, the Pakistani Muslim, Bangladeshi Muslim, Gujarati Hindus, Sikhs and the Whites, the process of 'self-segregation' has been quietly advancing over the last two decades or so. Each community has established their 'comfortable residential' zones. All Asian minority communities have avoided 'white estates' particularly council-owned properties. Factors such as 'ghetto security', nearness to families and friends, proximity to Asian social and religious facilities, availability of relatively cheap large houses, poverty and sheer inertia have contributed to 'self-segregation'. Discrimination in the housing market and of the housing finance lending institutions has also aided the fulfilment of 'ethnic preferences' in the choice of houses being bought. A dire consequence of segregation has been that the 'race' and 'religious' divide continues to deepen, sharpen and increase in bitterness. A lesson to learn from the Belfast comparison is to do whatever it is necessary to, and do it fast, if we are to avoid a spiralling cycle of hatred and violence.

Differences Between the 1995 and the 2001 Race Riots

* ❖ The involvement of white youths in the riots on the estates was a new dimension. Therefore, Bradford's racial tensions need to be analysed and understood from their aspect too.

* ❖ The sheer scale of the riots and the use of petrol bombs suggest that the violent acts were premeditated and pre-planned. Thus, the magnitude of damage was unimaginably greater.

140

❖ The rumours of the BNP coming to the city in large numbers and by the actual presence of a small number of supporters of the BNP close to the Anti-Nazi League rally in the city centre provided initial incitement and provocation to the rioters.

❖ For the first time, people across the political and religious spectrum publicly acknowledged that in Bradford it isn't an 'Asian' or a 'race relations' problem, it is a 'Muslim' problem or more precisely it is the problem of some Pakistani / Azad Kashmiri young people involved in a variety of political and anti-social activities. Like the Manningham riots of 1995, no Hindu, Sikh or African-Caribbean youths were involved in the violent clashes with the police or in burning, smashing and looting during the weekend of 7th and 8th July. A number of white correspondents writing in the local press used terms such as 'Muslim racism' and 'colonization by Muslims' to explain the behaviour of the Muslim youths who were involved.

❖ Little weight has been given to social deprivation amongst the causes of the riots.

❖ The TV and other media reporting the situation presented a horrendous image of the violence and terrifying experience of local residents, Asian and white. The media also carried comments of a much wider and stronger condemnation by community leaders and commentators than ever before. There was a strong and forthright condemnation of the Muslim youth involved in the riots by the leaders of their own community. For instance a group of 20 Asian businesses placed a full-page statement in the Telegraph & Argus (11 July 2001) to say "sorry for riots". The residents of Oak Lane, Heaton, White Abbey Road, Manchester Road and Manningham published an open letter (T&A, 11 July 2001) stating their unreserved condemnation of the horrific violence perpetrated by mindless Asian youths on the provocation of equally mindless supporters of the National Front.

❖ Contrary to the 1995 situation, most of the 13 elected Muslim councillors (4 Conservative and 9 Labour) in the city made little or only low profile comments on the havoc and devastation caused by the riots in their own wards. However, all MPs, including Marsha

141

Singh, expressed their sheer disgust with the behaviour of some of their constituents.

❖ Unlike the riots of 1995 there was no local public demand for the establishment of an enquiry or a commission by the Government to investigate the causes of riots. The Government viewed the situation as a 'local law and order issue' and condemned rioting as acts of "criminal thuggery" by a tiny minority of local youth "destroying their own community". It also rejected the call from the London-based Muslim Council of Britain to the Home Office to hold a Lord Scarman-type inquiry (Brixton Riots in 1981) into the riots in Bradford, Oldham and Burnley. However the Home Secretary did set up two groups to investigate the problems relating to community cohesion, rather lack of it, in these cities and invited suggestions for future public policy. The reports of both groups are discussed in chapter16.

❖ Despite some initial criticism of the police for their lack of adequate preparation, and their laissez-faire and/or overbearing approach in controlling the crowd, their actions were almost universally applauded. The police performance received a message of commendation from the Queen, too. The police's determination to restore calm and peace to the streets got the Home Secretary, David Blunkett's, unreserved appreciation and support.

❖ The Muslim community is asked to help root out the culprits and the perpetrators and hand them over to the police. The Pakistan High Commission in Britain and the Bradford Muslims' Professional Network, whilst condemning the rioters, strongly pleaded with the parents of the rioters to hand-over their youngsters to the police. After the police published the photographs of 20 youngsters wanted in connection with the crimes committed during the riots, amazingly quite a few surrendered themselves and a few parents contacted the police voluntarily about their own sons' involvement in the riots. This was a fairly unexpected response from Asian community members.

15

THE OUSELEY REPORT: REFLECTION AND ACTION

> **Community Pride not prejudice:**
> Making Diversity Work in Bradford
> *Presented to Bradford Vision by Sir Herman Ouseley*
>
> July 2001

After the demise of the BREC in the early part of 2000, Bradford Council held two consultation meetings with a group of people representing a wide range of interests in order to discuss the race relations situation in the city. The big question for the consultations was: "Why is community fragmentation along social, cultural, ethnic and religious lines occurring in the Bradford District?" As a result of these consultations the Council in collaboration with Bradford Vision set up the Bradford Race Review under the chairmanship of Sir Herman Ouseley in November 2000, primarily to find an answer to this question. The objective of the review was "to identify how public and private sector organisations, the voluntary sector and individuals can contribute towards greater understanding, respect and tolerance between all communities to enhance the social and economic regeneration of all these communities."

The Review Panel was given the following terms of reference:

(a) *To identify issues of shared concern and understanding in order to facilitate the building of bridges between communities where they do not exist and build and strengthen where they are weak and do not exist.*

(b) *To identify those issues that cause conflict and lead to polarisation between individuals and communities on the grounds of race, culture and religion and suggest methods for resolution.*

The struggle for racial justice

(c) To identify methods of working that will assist key institutions in the public, private and voluntary sectors, including faith organisations to create ownership and responsibility in promoting greater understanding and respect between communities.

(d) To consider whether a racial equality organisation is needed within the District and if so identify the role, structure and remit of such an organisation.

A set of principles expected that the Panel will:

1) pursue its task in depth and with breadth and seek to engage all communities with a variety of appropriate methods within the District;

2) be honest and open in its approach and that in the conduct of its work will open new relationships and dialogue between different communities, and will seek out examples of both good practice and poor practice and use these to shape recommendations;

3) have an open and transparent way of working and be accountable; and

4) acknowledge that not all its findings and recommendations will be agreeable to everyone who participates in the process.

After a considerable delay the report of the panel was formally published on 12 July, 2001.

In the wake of the Bradford riots Mike Priestley (T&A, 21 July 2001) wrote:

"It's the sort of relief you feel when a boil bursts and the pressure is released. The poison of political correctness which has debarred people from speaking their minds seems to have been washed away, at least for the time being. There has been a proper, free, fearless debate which has enabled the people of Bradford to confront the truth about a sorry situation in the city. Hopefully, that will now help us to start to deal with it."

144

Priestley used these words to commend comprehensive, free, fair and an overall superb coverage of the riots by the Telegraph and Argus. However, these words could be equally applicable to the publication of the findings of the Bradford Race Review on the state of race relations in Bradford.

Some commentators have remarked that, looked at broadly the report has not discovered anything new, entirely unknown, at least not to those involved with the race relations in the city. One senior local politician described the findings as "a sticking plaster applied to a grievous wound". (1) Nevertheless, the uniqueness of the report lies in reiterating the common concerns of most Bradfordians, white and the non-white, male and female, young and not-so-young, in an up-front manner. Its contribution became highly significant as its findings were leaked when Bradford was still busy clearing the wreckage of the riots from its streets prior to its official launch in full grandeur a couple of days later for the world media. Whilst the report sharpens the focus on the deep-seated ethnic diversity problems of Bradford; it also encourages the spirit of optimism amidst the chilling sensations of profound pessimism caused by its findings. At the same time as presenting a comprehensive compendium of Bradford's all-around problems, and the failure of its policies and leadership, it also highlights its strengths and some examples of good practices and projects in its attempts to foster harmonious relations between the diverse communities that live in the District. The review claims to be different in terms of seeking the views of those normally left out in most consultative exercises, that is, young people and women, especially from the black and minority ethnic communities (BMEC).

The broad blunt conclusions of the report include that "if the Bradford District is to meet its present challenges successfully it needs to act immediately to "initiate change to end racial self-segregation and cultural divisiveness", to "eliminate the culture of fear" and "create a 'can do' culture". The report also calls for the Muslim community to be prioritised in the economic regeneration of the city. It asserts, "if the Muslim community fails, Bradford fails".

Findings

The report highlights a large number of general concerns (2) and some significant issues regarding poor race relations in the District.

- An overall poor public image of Bradford is caused by the "white flight" and the movement out of the city by "middle class" people and by the Sikh and Hindu communities leaving behind an underclass of relatively poor white people, and visible minority ethnic communities with Muslim dominance.

- "Self-segregation is driven by fear of others, the need for safety from harassment and violent crime and the belief that it is the only way to promote, retain and protect faith and cultural identity and affiliation".

- "There is resentment towards the Asian community by sections of the white community, who perceive hostile and mono-cultural religious leaders as the advocates of segregation"

- "Political leadership has been weak in kowtowing to community leadership and operating within a 'doing deals' culture to avoid 'disturbances' and to 'keep the peace". The "so-called "community leaders" are self-styled, in league with the establishment key people and maintain the status quo of control and segregation through fear, ignorance and threats."

- "Community leaders tend to retain their power base by maintaining the segregated status quo, even when unrepresentative."

- There are common misconceptions and perceptions held by communities about each other. For example many white people believe that Muslims, particularly the Pakistanis, get everything and the rest get nothing. Likewise, Muslims assert that "Islamaphobia" and racism, which are prevalent in schools and community, "continue to blight their lives".

- "There is racism and racial discrimination in the labour market and in the workplace which limits equal opportunities for visible minority ethnic communities."

- There is lack of consultation with minority communities and their participation in mainstream social and educational activities is limited due to the marginalisation of minority ethnic teachers and governors, lack of knowledge of how the systems work, and the English language deficiency caused by 'inter-continental marriages'.

- "There is low level minority ethnic representation on decision-making bodies and executive boards with influence and impact." This is particularly the case with Asian women and young people.

- There is "the polarisation of communities along racial, ethnic and religious lines." There is: "virtual apartheid" in many secondary schools in the District; open racial conflict and harassment in and around schools; inadequate action by schools in dealing with racial incidents; a low level of academic achievement in too many schools; and under usage of inter-faith and intercultural studies facilities and resources.

- "There are conflicting styles of policing. Top-down management appear to push anti-racist approaches while rank and file officers remain fearful of being called racist and damaging their career prospects if they tackle black and Asian offenders".

- "Asian young men in gangs are alleged to boast that the police would not dare touch them for the fear they would 'riot' and people from all sections of the community resent the police for what they see as 'nothing being done against criminals'."

- There is blatant and open peddling of drugs in the inner city. " Police know who the drug pushers are but, as long as the drugs are peddled within the inner city and white suburbia is safe, they will do little or nothing".

The struggle for racial justice

The report says very boldly that the city finds itself "in the grip of fear", having lost its "spirit of community togetherness", and is witnessing "growing divisions among its population along race, ethnic, religious and social class lines". People suffer from the fear of:

> ➤ talking openly and honestly about problems, either within their communities or across different cultural communities, because of possible repercussions, recriminations and victimisation.

> ➤ leading and managing effective change because of possible public and media criticism.

> ➤ challenging wrong-doing because of being labelled "racist" - and that applies across all ethnic groups.

> ➤ crime even though the police say that violent crimes are on the decline.

> ➤ confronting the gang culture, the illegal drugs trade and the growing racial intolerance, harassment and abuse that exists.

> ➤ confronting all white and/or all Muslim schools about their contribution, or rather lack of contribution, to social and racial integration.

> ➤ establishing a corporate identity for the District as a whole as most people outside the city and immediate surrounds do not see themselves as part of Bradford.

The report stresses that if Bradford District is to meet successfully the challenges posed by its present circumstances and its uniqueness, there has to be immediate action to initiate change to end racial self-segregation and cultural divisiveness. The first priority for the District's leaders is to create a "can do" culture and to eliminate the culture of fear. It recognises that there will be "no gain without pain".

The report emphasises the need for "a powerful unifying vision for the District and strong political, municipal and community leadership". It also stresses a desperate need to launch an all inclusive " People Programme that creates social harmony, rejects racial hatred, brings communities together and shows them how to value people of all backgrounds." In moving forward, the report proposes a bold Bradfordian People Programme (3) with the following four features:

Citizenship Education embracing the theme of citizenship in its schools, building on the national initiative to ensure that all young people learn about diversity and the need to respect people from all social, religious and cultural backgrounds.

A Centre for Diversity, Learning and Living a centre of excellence focusing on all the people of Bradford District and the means by which they can share their diverse experiences. It would provide expertise, advice and guidance for all the District's institutions and organisations on a range of issues including inter-faith/cultural studies, anti-discrimination activities and best practice. It would also provide support and advice for individuals in discrimination or racial harassment cases.

Behavioural Competency Framework for the Workplace with the aim to encourage all organisations to ensure that, their staff are aware of the District's many different social, cultural and religious communities and their particular needs. It would outline 'standards of behaviour' for employees and to ensure that workers and workplaces demonstrate and reflect an enhanced understanding and experience of the District's diversity.

Equality and Diversity Contract Conditions in order to promote social and cultural mixing as well as good race relations, equality and diversity conditions should be inserted in all contracts of grant-aid, public-financed investments, all supplies and contracted services as well as in partnership projects / programmes.

Some Observations
In the wake of the riots and the findings of the Race Review Panel a question mark has been placed on the way the official promotion of

'multiculturalism' in Bradford may have contributed to the present tensions. When minority ethnic cultures are celebrated in a high profile manner (particularly in schools) white people may naturally wonder what theirs amounts to. Melanie Phillips (The Times, 3 June 2001) argues that "this anxiety over cultural invisibility drives some whites to identify with racist political groups. And it's the people who have the least emotional resilience, and who therefore feel most insecure, who are most likely to be receptive to racist extremism".

In the spatially segregated communities, and with the situation of 'virtual apartheid' in many local schools, multiculturalism in practice so far has proved divisive. In the interest of 'equality' and 'egalitarianism' only the ethnic cultures and social norms of the BMEC have been promoted which has led to tribalism. It appears that the results of preaching 'inclusiveness' have ironically produced 'exclusiveness'. 'White flight' from the inner city ethnic concentrations and the emergence of white 'no-go' areas seem to be a natural outcome. A good deal of the white resentment of non-whites is based on the perception that ethnic issues get prominence and therefore attract more resources to redress them. This causes tensions based on the perception of unfairness and preferential treatment.

Bradford suffers from racism and Islamaphobia. These result in harassment, discrimination and exclusion. Disturbances on the street perpetuate and deepen these features even further. Whilst riots may be the Muslim youths' reaction to white racism and Islamaphobia, in turn, they also harden the existing negative stereotypes further. It is a vicious circle.

Trans-continental marriages, in which one partner is likely to be non-English speaking, have been identified as a source of concern to British born young Asians (particularly girls), and a detriment to the educational achievement of Asians in schools and the development of harmonious inter-community relations. Despite some obvious negative impacts of such marriages on the social and economic progress and prosperity of the families involved, this pattern of marriages is likely to continue for the foreseeable future particularly among the Muslim communities. And any attempts to hinder the contracting of such marriages are likely to be strongly opposed on grounds of human rights and race equality.

The Bradford experience suggests that religious schools, despite their high academic achievement and good discipline, may not be a good option for the city. The Government policy to increase the number of grant-aided denominational schools will raise expectations amongst the South Asian communities to set up their own schools and thus add to the serious 'exclusiveness' that already exists.

The proposed Bradfordian People Programme offers a number of sound initiatives worth a trial. However, for the success of the 'People Programme' the leadership must "engage, harness, use and value the talents and abilities of all sections of the District's diverse cultural communities". The programme must be "dialogue-driven" and communication must "convince local people of the benefits to be gained from the District's diverse cultural, ethnic, faith and multi-lingual communities and, to do so through interacting and working together." It must build on the local strengths and upon the experience of many sound projects that are already in progress in the city.

Above all, those responsible for planning, designing, implementing and monitoring the Programme, must learn from the successes and failures of policies and programmes from the 1980s. I believe there are lessons to be learnt. (4)

16

COMMUNITY COHESION: A BUZZWORD FOR FUTURE RACE RELATIONS

The struggle for racial justice in Britain is an on going movement and is likely to continue for many more decades to come. The persistence of racism, racial prejudice, and social and economic inequalities combined with a range of strongly differing cultural, religious and linguistic traditions make British society inherently unstable, incoherent and divisive. Therefore, a regular review of local and national official strategies underpinning public policy measures becomes essential if social disorders of the kind experienced in 2001 are to be avoided and some cohesion within diverse communities is to be achieved and then sustained.

In an immediate government response to the social disorders of last summer (2001) the Home Secretary set up two separate groups to study the circumstances leading to the riots in three affected northern cities, Bradford, Burnley and Oldham. The Ministerial Group was established "to examine and consider how national policies might be used to promote better community cohesion, based upon shared values and a celebration of diversity." The second group, Community Cohesion Review Team (CCRT) chaired by Ted Cantle was "to seek the views of local residents and community leaders in the affected towns and in other parts of England on the issues which need to be addressed to bring about social cohesion and also to identify good practice in handling of these issues at local level."

The reports of these two groups were published simultaneously in December 2001 under the titles: *Building Cohesive Communities: A Report of the Ministerial Group on Public Order and Community Cohesion*; and *Community Cohesion: A Report of the Independent Review Team.* (1)

The report of the (CCTR) sets out what they found in the places they visited. It presents a thoughtful analysis of a wide range of issues in a narrative form under fourteen themes ranging from people, education, housing, regeneration strategies, political and community leadership to policing and the media. The analysis of major concerns is accompanied by 67 recommendations for action which the Team consider will improve community cohesion and help address some of the factors which lay behind the disturbances earlier in the year. The report acknowledges that the Team "did not try to assess the problems and pose solutions for each area separately, it was however possible to identify common threads and good practices". A summary of the Team's findings about these common features of the areas that experienced disorders are neatly noted on pages 8-9 of the Ministerial Group Report. In general the CCTR report supports and echoes the findings of the Ouseley Report on Bradford. The Cantle Report claims that its set of practical recommendations "should act as a steer to what needs to be done in the future." The Ministerial Group report contains the government action taken so far and proposals for further action.

As the titles of both reports suggest, "community cohesion" (2) is the new buzzword running through these reports. CCTR stresses "an urgent need to promote community cohesion based on a greater knowledge of, contact between, and respect for, the various cultures that now make Great Britain such a rich and diverse nation."

The report also underscores the necessity " to establish a greater sense of citizenship, based on (a few) common principles which are shared and observed by all sections of the community. This concept of citizenship would also place a higher value on cultural differences." It stresses that these shared principles of citizenship should be developed through a wide "national debate, heavily influenced by younger people". The report recognises that "white" as well as ethnic minority communities' have a problem of tiptoeing "around the sensitive issues of race, religion and culture" with the fear of falling foul of political correctness. Therefore the debate needs to be honest and open about the positive values of diversity, led by the government and with a heavy involvement of the younger generation.

The struggle for racial justice

The Ministerial Report acknowledges that the "government cannot create community cohesion. It is something that communities must do themselves with Government's help as enabler and supporter." It advocates that community cohesion should be achieved through locally developed plans and a programme of 'myth busting'. The government is expecting the local authorities in Bradford, Burnley and Oldham to publish their plans for community cohesion by April 2002. The report also recommends the establishment of "a new Community Cohesion Task Force" to oversee the development of local community cohesion strategies and the implementation of its recommendations.

These reports stress the responsibility of local political leaders to work towards making community cohesion a reality. They also highlight that the full strength of the new Race Relations (Amendment) Act 2000 should be utilised in innovative and imaginative ways to tackle racism at all levels including problems such as Islamaphobia and disaffection within certain sections of communities.

Both reports stress in no uncertain terms that making English the common first language of all citizens is a fundamental step towards achieving community cohesion and for shaking the foundations of a complex phenomenon of 'self-segregation'. In a prelude speech to the publication of these two reports the Home Secretary proposed that a reasonable command of English should be made a precondition for acquiring British citizenship.

These reports also acknowledge that the multiplicity of government and local initiatives aimed at fighting racial disadvantage have so far ensured divisions instead. The reports warn that local government has to look at councillors offering "sweetheart" deals with self-appointed community leaders. The basic criteria for allocating cash in regeneration scheme projects should be a particular group's need rather than its ethnicity.

Creating community cohesion has to be a two-way street, the white community taking responsibility for eradicating racism and valuing living in a multicultural society; and the minority communities instilling a sense of British citizenship.

The reports suggest that the police should use all the powers available to them within the existing legal framework to monitor and to deal with the activities of far right organisations and their members. The constructive role of the local press and the communities in identifying and supporting the police in apprehending those involved in the riots in Bradford is also a valuable lesson for the future.

The Ouseley and the Cantle reports provide ample evidence to challenge the popular belief that the second generation of the New Commonwealth immigrant communities would naturally learn English and would integrate within the wider British society more easily and in more ways than their parents. Their integration would be further facilitated with the gradual reduction in white prejudice and racism with the passage of time. These assumptions led to a generally reactive approach to race relations that has sought to address the consequences of white racism through anti-discrimination legislation and the promotion of equality of opportunity, and to minimise white prejudice through the promotion of multi-culturalism in its various forms.

Until the publication of these reports 'segregation' was rarely used in discussions of community relations in Britain. A complex set of factors such as the preferences of various minority groups to live closer together for cultural, religious and safety reasons and the discriminatory policies and practices of lending institutions and housing organisations have led to segregation in education and employment as well. The Cantle Report echoes the main findings of the Ouseley Report including the evident reality of some cities where white and minority communities operate on a series of "parallel lines". Physical segregation is compounded by separate education, social and cultural networks and employment. There is the suspicion of "postcode discrimination" in employment. Tackling segregation (widely assumed to be self-segregation) has now occupied a central position in the proposed approaches to race relations under the new concept of community cohesion.

The struggle for racial justice

Some recommendations in the reports are very difficult to implement and are likely to cause resentment and controversy. The recommendation for all faith schools to offer 25 per cent of places to pupils of other faiths and no faith is fraught with practical problems. For the non-faith schools to have a statutory duty to promote respect for, and an understanding of, the cultures in the school and neighbourhood in order to create a 'sense of belonging' in children from ethnic minorities through its curriculum is most unlikely to become more than an academic exercise. Likewise, the proposal about attempts to maintain a racial balance in all schools in areas of high concentration of minority communities is likely to open a fresh debate about 'bussing', which was declared a racially discriminatory policy in the 1970s.

Despite clear evidence of strong opposition to increasing the number of faith schools from the responses of sixty six national organisations presented in the Cantle Report (page 59), the Government's policy to encourage and support their establishment is difficult to appreciate. Given the situation of almost non-existent community cohesion in Bradford where the communities are deeply fractured along racial, religious and cultural lines, development of faith schools is likely to prove unhelpful for future race relations.

The Home Secretary, David Blunkett's, statements in the context of these reports explicitly question the validity of traditional wisdom in dealing with race issues in the country. He suggests an open debate to introduce a change in the direction of future race relations in Britain. As a part of his new approach he intends to introduce a clear shift in immigration policy and procedures, to make these more liberal and relevant to the needs of the economy. Such a change, he believes, would assist in managing more effectively the problem of asylum seekers, illegal immigration and some concerns about a thin flow of 'economic migrants' under the disguise of marriage partners.

Some of the Home Secretary's statements attracted an immediate negative reaction from various directions. For example, he suggested that "a modest grasp of English" and some sort of oath of allegiance to abide by British "norms of acceptability" should become a prerequisite of citizenship (on similar lines as the applicants for citizenship are required to do in the USA and Canada). Both suggestions attracted strong reactions from some of his own party members and Muslim leaders in particular. His insensitive choice of examples of forced marriages and female circumcision to make his point about "norms of acceptability" which must apply to recent immigrants and long-established communities alike led to unhelpful condemnations of his otherwise significant point about the equality of women's rights in a civilised society.

These proposals were described as 'patronising of minorities', 'insensitive', 'disturbing', 'not at all helpful', 'nonsense' and 'sensational'. Despite the choice of harsh words, the sentiments behind this criticism hold some validity. For instance, to describe all black and South Asian communities in Britain as "immigrant communities" is misleading, to make judgement about all minority cultures on the existence of some repugnant practices in certain sections of those communities is unwise, and to give the impression of suspecting the 'Britishness' and loyalty to Britain of minority communities is wrong and unacceptable. However the Home Secretary's blunt expression of proposals need to be understood in the context of the reports on extremely damaging and violent race riots in the country, and also at a time when a few Britons were alleged to be fighting in Afghanistan with al-Qaeda forces against British-backed forces.

In Bradford, the Home Secretary's statements and some of the recommendations in these reports brought a quick emotional negative reaction even from some younger community leaders. They tried to dismiss any linkage between the 'lack of English' and the involvement of young Muslims in riots. They also argued that the inability to understand English had no relevance to the existence of 'segregation' and had little impact on the perpetuation of social deprivation. Nevertheless it is a fact that a good standard in English helps in achieving higher educational qualifications which in turn influence career opportunities and, eventually, choices in the housing market. Indian and East-African minority communities, living and working in similar circumstances have integrated better, achieve higher standards in education, and have done well in employment and housing. In their cases a sound knowledge of English has proved a major contributory

157

factor to their quick progress from an immigrant position to that of successful members of the local community.

To weaken the current level of segregation and to foster community cohesion, traditional community leaders and local politicians have to stop being defensive and be bold enough to accept the uncomfortable realities of the local situation, and be more receptive to trying new ideas. The Ouseley and the Cantle reports see the positive commitment and loyalty of the younger population to Bradford, the city of their birth, as a reason for optimism in the future. It is this section of the local population from which the media and the institutions should look for the future community leaders and concentrate on cultivating their secular outlook and vision, and empowering them to bring about a sustainable change in the plight of their communities. At the same time, minority communities need to encourage young people to participate in the management of community affairs and create space for them in leadership roles.

17

FUTURE RACE RELATIONS IN BRADFORD: WHAT MATTERS (1)

Bradford is becoming a city of two separate worlds: a world of white people and another world composed of a few brown and black diverse communities with their own languages, cultures, religious beliefs, dress and food patterns. The division between these two worlds is becoming sharper and more visible. These two worlds freely and frequently meet only in the labour market using English as a medium of communication. Social interaction between these two worlds is confined to the presence of minority communities' recognised dignitaries at some civic and public functions or in the celebrations of community festivals such as Bradford Mela. The popularly cherished view of three decades ago that these two worlds would fuse into one, once the minority groups had passed through an initial short phase of adjustment, has proved a myth.

In Bradford, race relations are viewed largely in terms of South Asian communities versus the white population and most of the time even more narrowly as a 'Muslim problem' and no more. The discussion that follows primarily concentrates on the issues relating to the South Asian communities, that includes people of Indian, Pakistani and Bangladeshi ethnic origin but, it does not assume that the black Caribbean and African communities have no stake in the situation.

South Asian Visibility
In the 1980s, the local authority and other public sector institutions and voluntary agencies reluctantly replaced their policy objective of achieving assimilation by a more liberal practical objective of achieving pluralism through the introduction of policies such as multi-faith religious education in schools and equal opportunity policies in

employment. The measures taken under these policies do not seem to have facilitated the integration of South Asians into mainstream society. Nevertheless, the positive effects of these measures have heightened South Asians' own consciousness about their rights as equal citizens, and have helped them considerably to reaffirm and consolidate their cultural and religious identities. Now the South Asian communities in Bradford have a very high 'visible ethnic identity'. This high visibility of South Asian people, their cultures and institutions, is continuously reinforcing the white population's fear of being swamped by foreigners and their alien value systems. Such fears are a permanent threat to harmonious community or race relations.

Another aspect of the South Asian population is its relatively large size and concentration in inner-city areas. According to Bradford Council's estimate the total black and Asian population of Bradford is set to rise from around 96,000 in 2000 to 138,900 by 2011. In some inner city wards there is a very high concentration of South Asians. For example, according to the Census 1991 data, the University ward had more than 68% South Asians and almost 50 % of the population of Bradford Moor and Toller wards was of South Asian origin. Within these wards there is high concentrations of particular ethnic groups as well. Fifty two per cent of the University, and 45 % of Toller and 37 % of Bradford Moor wards' people were of Pakistani origin. (2) Similarly, three quarters of all Bangladeshis lived in the Cornwall Road area of Manningham and in inner Keighley with a further concentration in Bowling Ward.

Communities Within Communities

In Britain today, the notion of an 'Asian' community being a homogeneous single entity is misleading. Indians of East African origin are quite differently placed in terms of their economic position and success in Britain. Even among the individual communities such as Pakistani Muslims, a clear distinction can be made between those who come from the Punjab region and those who migrated from the Azad Kashmir area in their life styles, standard of living and attitude to integration and so on. The reality is that different groups are developing their common distinctive identities only in 'religious beliefs and practices'.

A deepening polarisation of Bradford's minority communities on religious lines is a cause for serious concern over the perpetuation of tensions between and within the South Asian communities. Incidents of damage to property and malicious attacks on religious buildings have been witnessed quite a few times in the city in the past. Such sharp religious divisions may also lead to the use of the religious card in local politics. For example, a leaflet written in Urdu and English urged Muslims in Bradford Moor not to vote for the Labour Party candidate, Raghvir Virdee, in the 1995 May elections, because he was a Sikh / Hindu. In 1997, in the adoption of the Labour party candidate for the Bradford West Parliamentary constituency, Marsha Singh's rival Muslim candidates were accused of striking a secret deal among themselves to put a solid opposition to his adoption by agreeing on one Muslim name.

South Asian Community Leadership

The experience of Bradford since the beginning of the 1990s suggests that the notion of 'community leaders' is almost a redundant idea. The concept of 'community leaders' or 'community elders' is only relevant in the context of small 'homogeneous groups' in villages in the Indian sub-continent where life is still organised and social control is exercised through patriarchal cultural norms and values. In Bradford, outwardly 'close knit' looking South Asian communities are internally quite heterogeneous in composition. They have their community-wide known and respected personalities but they do not carry the traditional position of influence and social control, especially upon the younger generation whose members quite often operates beyond their narrow social group boundaries. This was very clearly demonstrated when so-called community leaders were shouted down and heckled when they tried to mediate between the police and Muslim youths involved in the Manningham riots in 1995. Justifiably, South Asian youngsters may feel no traditional obligation to and reverence for those leaders who they believe neither understand their problems nor have taken any positive steps to address their issues or concerns. Thus, it is wrong to assume that the community or community leaders are losing control over the youth. The existence of any such control has always been a myth. The findings of the Ouseley Report lend further support to this view.

The young people present at the scene of the disturbances seriously questioned the leadership of the Asian elected councillors. They publicly accused the elected councillors of using their positions for self-advancement and for ignoring young people's particular problems. The concern is genuinely felt. There had been robust expression of disappointment in the recent reports on race relations in the city on the lack of vision by local politicians about dealing with race inequalities. This is even more so about the South Asian elected leaders. The elected councillors from minority communities are capable of adding different and valuable perspectives to add to the policies to the normal (largely white) perspective of the political parties to which they belong, simply because of their first-hand knowledge and experience of being a member of ethnic minority groups themselves. There is very little evidence to suggest that the South Asian politicians have successfully acted as opinion makers on wider issues or in leading their communities. Their role in fostering good community relations has also been unclear and limited so far. Despite the fact that there are a dozen elected South Asian councillors to speak on behalf of their communities, very few are believed to have represented their communities effectively.

Politics is about clash of alternative visions about society and approaches to social issues. As race issues are always hypersensitive, councillors from ethnic minority background may feel inhibited to speak their mind to avoid causing conflict within their own political group or an offence to the party leadership and their colleagues by making a dissenting voice. The dissent that may affect his/her *individual* interest and future within the political group. Nevertheless, a healthy debate should not be stifled on a significant cause such race relations, simply for the sake of party political line. Thus more courage and honesty is expected from the ethnic minority councillors if racial inequalities are to be reduced.

White Politicians

Politicians are expected to be visionary in order to offer set of political principles for the civil servants to deliver. Leading politicians who normally chair committees must be competent managers in addition to them being visionary. In the field of race relations the challenge for local politicians is extraordinary. On the one hand they are expected to address the diverse needs of employment and social mobility for minority groups and to meet their genuine expectations for a position of respect, dignity and social status. They also have to be responsive to the religious sensibilities of the minority ethnic communities. On the other hand, they need to avoid with care the accusation of providing privileged treatment to ethnic minority groups. In dealing with racial inequality issues cross-party political consensus and co-operation may be essential, but it may weaken the clarity and passion of a political edge generally required to controversial issues such as race relations. Furthermore, politicians from the more affluent districts may feel less obliged to deliver the promises or commitments made by their party leaders, as their political success does not rest on ethnic votes. Not to mention the misguided interests or political opportunists all too ready to take advantage of any collapse of harmonious race relations in the city.

The Honeyford affair in the 1980s demonstrated clearly that white politicians sympathetic to South Asian issues found it problematic to provide a successful leadership to the South Asian groups in their fight for racial justice and in redressing their particular problems. At times the South Asians suspected their sincerity, and their own white colleagues simply ignored them for being 'political opportunists'.

South Asian Youth
The younger generation of South Asian communities, particularly the Muslim youth, has only become starkly visible through its size and specific needs during the last ten to fifteen years. The nature and intensity of their concerns is quite different from those of their parents. Unemployment, for example, supported by welfare payments is less worrying and frustrating to a man with little transferable skills and qualifications than to a young educated qualified man or a woman with higher career expectations to succeed in his/ her life. The investments made in the family land or houses in Mirpur, Sylhet or Punjab are no consolation to a young person aspiring to live in a decent house, drive a good car and enjoy the other comforts of life in Bradford. The parental logic behind such investments no longer appeals to their children. They feel that many parents have made little investment in their children to enable them to exploit their full potential to succeed in life and enjoy a higher standard of living in the UK.

The struggle for racial justice

There is no real evidence to suggest that young South Asians have lost respect for their parents and that the social and moral fabric of the South Asian family is disintegrating. Their respect for the immediate family has changed little but the extended social networks based on caste, clans, regional loyalties, etc. have little relevance for them in the British context.

South Asian young people expect to enjoy many of the things which their local white counterparts enjoy as a matter of normality. They are re-defining their cultural and religious values in relation to western standards and values. They aspire to more freedom in the choice of education, careers, friends and marriage and political activities. It is in these contexts that they see the broad ethnic social networks, including their parents', as obstructive barriers. The majority of them have learnt to negotiate successfully with their parents, with tact, patience and persistence on most of these issues. However, they have no experience or skills to equip them to deal with so-called community leaders.

There appears to be an increasing awareness among Muslim youth about the territorial ownership of their residential areas such as Manningham, West Bowling and Thornbury. It is a unique and a very different awareness from that of their parents, who always felt and behaved like sojourners. The strategies of young Muslims to deal with local issues, therefore, contrast and conflict with those of their parents. For them those areas are their world in which their cultural, social, religious or moral ethos should prevail uninterrupted. For example, the visibly flourishing trade in sex and drugs is seen as a threat to the moral fabric of the local Muslim community. It is ironic that four decades ago the indigenous community felt the same about the swamping of their culture by the growing presence of South Asians and the emergence of their own social infrastructure. The exclusion strategies of harassment and collusion currently being adopted by Muslim youths in places like Oldham and Bradford don't seem to be dissimilar to those of anti-immigrant groups operating in the 1960s. Youths on white housing estates in Bradford have shown similar tendencies during the July 2001 riots.

The nature of the militancy and the politicisation of South Asian youths first evidenced by the *Bradford 12* in 1981 seem to have changed. The co-operation between Asian youths across religious boundaries has disappeared. Religious issues seem to have taken priority over more general but serious concerns about discrimination, deprivation and social justice. It is important for the local policy makers to recognise that such bigger issues should not be ignored or given a lower priority over such religious concerns, however, important those may be for the individual religious communities.

At the time of the appointment of the first Muslim advisor to the Prison Service in September 1999 the Home Office reported that the number of Muslim prisoners in British jails had doubled over the last years and their number was expected to increase sharply. Almost one third of the Muslim prisoners in 1997 were serving sentences for violence and sex offences, 22 % for drugs, 12 % for robbery and 10 % for theft and fraud. Manawar Jan-Khan, an official of the Manningham Residents' Association, expressing the concerns of Muslim youth at the time of the Manningham riots in 1995 commented: "We have seen a dramatic change of attitude among young Asian people. They are more westernised...they will drink alcohol and go to clubs. There are young people selling drugs because it is lucrative and is an easy option. If you are a kid on the streets of Bradford with no job, you look at what hope you got; what your friends are doing; who you hang about with", plays a part in the drug related crime. (The Times, September 3, 1999) It is also interesting to note the findings of the Powerful Whispers (3) in Little Horton that Asian families in particular were profoundly embarrassed at the possibility of their children being drawn into neighbourhood criminality.

South Asian Girls
The predicament of South Asian girls has regularly attracted the attention of local as well as national media. Most of the time the dilemma they face arises from the cultural and religious practices of their own communities. Nevertheless, their problems have also become a serious concern of local politicians, teachers and social workers, and from time to time have affected cross-community relations in the city adversely. For example, right through the period 1960 to the middle of

The struggle for racial justice

the 1980s, Muslim girls missing from Bradford schools remained one of the major issues in education. For instance, the Directorate of Educational Services in the city suggested a figure of 500 girls missing from schools in 1983. There were two explanations of this situation. (a) In the early years of immigration more Pakistani families brought their boys over to Britain than girls. Many parents left their girls behind with grandparents or close relatives. (b) A significant number of Muslim girls were either kept at home (illegally withdrawn from schools) or sent back to Pakistan at puberty by their parents without any information being given to the schools. Whilst these absences were considered legitimate by Muslim parents, they proved a serious concern to the education and social services officials.

An issue that remained a cause for concern for all South Asian parents and caused serious tension between Muslim and Hindu/Sikh communities, related to Asian girls being met by Asian boys and sometimes by Asian taxi drivers (who were largely Muslim) outside school gates. The parents accused schools and the police of doing very little, if anything at all, to stop the harassment of their daughters. Contrary to the serious concerns of the South Asian parents the view of teachers and police was that it was a normal part of the experience of growing up in a western environment.

The media have always been attracted to the cultural practice of 'arranged marriages' among South Asian communities. The practice of 'arranged marriages' was commonly presented as 'forced marriages'. It cannot be denied that some 'forced marriages' do take place and some 'arranged marriages' break down for a variety of reasons. In recent years, South Asian girls leaving home from the fear of pressure from their parents to agree to unacceptable marriage arrangements proposed by their parents have been getting regular headlines. For example, according to the Telegraph & Argus (January 20, 2001) the number of cases of 'runaway women' dealt with by West Yorkshire police increased from 144 in 1995 to 206 in 1997 and has stabilised around 280 each year for 1999 and 2000. Whatever the magnitude of the problem it reflects negatively on the development of positive esteem for South Asian cultures; whilst equality of respect and status for all

166

cultures is a prerequisite for good community relations. The Muslim community's image in the city suffers more from such stories in the press than do other ethnic communities.

This becomes a major race relations issue when "AGONY OF THE RUNAWAY BRIDES" becomes the front cover headline of the local paper that devotes pages and pages to the subject for five consecutive days (Telegraph & Argus, 27-31, October 1998). The Times' comment column (March 4, 2000) remarked that "forced marriages are among the commonest abuses of human rights in Britain" and the Government set up a working party, headed by two Asian peers, to study the problem and suggest remedies. However, the fact remains that the whole process of marriage arrangements in South Asian communities has undergone a tremendous change. Most marriages are now 'mutually agreed choices between parents and their children'.

The 500-600 'international marriages' contracted between the British-born Muslim young people and their spouses from the sub-continent each year have an indirect impact on race inequalities too. There are two predictable consequences of these marriages: (a) Within the Muslim community the home culture and home language is likely to remain other than English requiring language support for the children and thus slowing down the whole process of their adjustment in the wider society. (b) It increases the likelihood of the continuation of many more "unstable and unhappy" marriages.

South Asian Under-Class
Ethnicity in itself does not constitute material disadvantage. However, the minority ethnic communities in the city suffer relatively more from multiple deprivation than the white population. For instance, over 53% of Pakistani, 81% of Bangladeshi, 43% Afro-Caribbean and 25% Indian residents in Bradford, compared with only 20% of the whole population lived in areas of multiple deprivation. Little Horton and University wards, with high concentration of South Asian population, have consistently high mortality rates, one third above the national average and they have double the percentage of low-birth weight babies born compared to the rural wards. (4)

The struggle for racial justice

Again, a very high proportion of households with no one in employment were in the areas of South Asian concentration, University (50.4%), Bradford Moor (44.8%), Bowling (44.7%), Little Horton (51.4%), Undercliffe (41.6%), Toller (40.9%) and Heaton (36.7%), compared with the District average of 37.5 per cent. (5) In all these areas the individuals receiving community charge rebate in 1992 were at least 10 % higher than the District average of 25 per cent. Children receiving free meals in first schools in Bradford Moor, Bowling, Little Horton and University were 56%, 45%, 44% and 39 % respectively, compared with the District average of 30 per cent. (6)

A local study found that whilst 19.5% of the general population lived in the areas of multiple stress, 25% of Indians, 42.7% of African-Caribbean, 53.2 % of Pakistanis and 81% of Bangladeshi residents lived in the multiple stress areas. (7) In addition to this, high crime rate areas are in the inner-city district too. Particularly for the Muslim communities, high mortality and proportion of births of low-weight babies are a significant health issue. These statistics are clear and convincing evidence of poverty and an emerging under class position for Pakistani and Bangladeshi communities in the city.

Poverty and general deprivation among South Asians in Bradford is likely to become more evident and acute in the coming years for a variety of reasons. The income of South Asian families is likely to remain low and perhaps even decline. Unemployment rates among South Asians are high. According to the 1991 Census, among ethnic minorities, as many as two out of every three 16-24 year olds were unemployed. A TUC report has pointed out that unemployment among Bradford's black and Asian populations is the worst in the country. (8) Bradford needs 700 new jobs each year just to maintain employment at its current level. In the next decade there will be a substantial increase in the number of 19-24 years old in the ethnic minority population and therefore any increase in unemployment will naturally fall on young ethnic minorities. It is estimated that between 1991-2011, the net increase in workforce by ethnic group will be as follows: 7,000 Pakistani, 650 Bangladeshi and 850 Indian. (9) This does not present any hope for additional South Asian job seekers and for those who are currently unemployed.

Increased self-employment among South Asians has to some extent cushioned the negative effects of structural changes in the local labour market, particularly for middle aged men in some sections of the community. However, this route may not be either available or even a preferred option for most young people. Even for the first generation, self-employment, particularly in the retailing sector, is a struggle for survival.

Bradford has seen a significant change in the structure of the local labour market, that is, a shift from manufacturing to service industries. Locally, most of the new jobs are created in retailing, financial services and modern technology. Education and training need to prepare young people for jobs in these new areas of future development. Unless ethnic minority young people are encouraged by their parents to consider a bigger diversity in their traditional pattern of career choices they are likely to lose out. It appears that young people based in the suburbs are better equipped to fill these jobs than their peers in the inner city. In view of the movement of such services, particularly retailing, to the outskirts, incomes earned from the city centre areas are most likely to be spent further away from the centre, causing a further dent in the regeneration of the inner city economy.

The South Asian communities, particularly the Pakistani and Bangladeshi communities, have not fully recognised the changes in the local labour market which have affected their employment opportunities so drastically. Their young people have to be prepared and perhaps encouraged to seek jobs further afield. Most of the young professionally qualified Hindus and Sikhs are increasingly doing so already. Therefore, any barriers, social or otherwise, need to be removed to facilitate the mobility of young people. External constraints inhibiting mobility may be beyond the control of the South Asian communities but parents and community leaders can certainly liberalise their own thinking particularly about social and religious obligations such as arranged marriages which put intense pressure on young people to stay close by.

The struggle for racial justice

There is a declining demand for non-English speaking female labour locally. It is likely to reduce employment opportunities for South Asian women and, subsequently, their contribution to family incomes. Eventually a very high proportion of South Asians in the inner city may have their entire income coming from state benefits which are likely to be lower than the income from full time employment in most cases.

The extended family in the traditional sense is on its way out. As a consequence the size of the disposable income available to a household is likely to be reduced. Furthermore, the establishment of independent family units by younger people whose consumption patterns is very close to that of their western counterparts would add to household expenditure. The proportion of aged members in South Asian households is rapidly increasing, with the cost of their support and care proving greater than the income their presence may add to the family budget.

One long-term consequence of the ethnic or racial disturbances on the streets of Bradford is likely to be a decline in investment in the inner city generally and in the areas of ethnic concentrations specifically. The selective nature of the attacks during the Manningham riots of 1995 and the July 2001 riots when non-Muslim businesses suffered significantly greater damage, exacerbated inter-community tensions. Making non-Muslim communities feel insecure in areas of Muslim concentrations is likely to worsen the already underclass position of Pakistani and Bangladeshi communities in the city.

Challenges

Dealing with frequent street disturbances is one of the major challenges for Bradford. Past experience shows that once the dust of a major street disturbance settles the interest in the inner city problem wanes. This gives the depressing impression that all elected politicians, including South Asian councillors and community representatives, pursue only their own selfish motives to make whatever small capital they can from the unfortunate social upheaval. However, it is vital to encourage an on-going debate on the current reality, so that the issues of discrimination, deprivation, cultural and religious diversity and fair treatment can be discussed honestly and constructively. The truth may be unpalatable and even uncomfortable for all sides to accept.

Simply blaming institutional and structural factors such as white racism and economic decline for all individual and social ills is neither appropriate nor justified. For the resolution of inner-city social disorders and deprivation, there is a general tendency to expect action by official agencies such as the police, the local authority and even from the majority community. Sadly, this is usually without any specific reference to the role of the local South Asian communities in the deprived areas. Such an omission assumes that either these communities are totally incapable, helpless or powerless to do anything about their plight or, worse, that they do not even matter. Both these assumptions are incorrect and damaging to the future of these communities. It can be argued that they have an equally, if not more, important role to play. A good deal of responsibility for the current level of deprivation, youth alienation and lack of opportunities needs to be shared between parents, so called community leaders and local politicians, and, of course in the wider context, the Government's economic policies and other initiatives.

South Asian communities can contribute effectively in diminishing the impact of serious inner-city issues in a variety of ways. For example, minority communities can make a considerable contribution to the debate about the issues of racial inequalities and to the fulfilment of any action plans to alleviate them. They are closer to the issues than anybody else and they have more to gain or lose from the success or failure of initiatives which the authorities may undertake to redress these inequalities on their behalf. These communities do have internal resources both financial and human which once redirected can have a real impact in reducing social inequalities. It is not suggested that community resources should replace state funding for various activities but that they should complement those resources. There is an increasing pool of professional people within ethnic minority groups currently working with local institutions who can pro-actively engage in a voluntary capacity to assist in raising their own communities awareness and in dealing with the issues of racial inequality and community relations.

The struggle for racial justice

In the field of education parents may not be able to contribute to the improvement of failing school buildings or the reduction in class sizes but they can certainly help in reducing the truancy rate and in increasing the proportion of children leaving schools with some qualifications. Currently, Bradford schools are among the worst in the country for pupils playing truant. Bradford is also at the lowest end of the school performance League Tables of local education authorities in relation to the proportion of children leaving schools with qualifications (at 95th position, with 15.4 % lower than the England average). It does not require any imagination to realise that for the inner city schools, which the majority of the South Asian children attend, the figures are even worst. (10) Furthermore, over 30 per cent of Bradford's current school population enter schools with English as their second, third or fourth language. (11)

The South Asian communities are not fully aware about the limitations of the 'dependency culture', the reliance on the welfare state and state financial handouts for community development and regeneration projects. Regular special pleadings by local politicians for additional resources to deal with the disadvantages of ethnic minority communities are unlikely to get more cash into their begging bowls irrespective of the political colour of future governments. Therefore, self-help and self-reliance in dealing with their own deprivation and pro-active initiatives in developing strong networks with other voluntary and public sector agencies are the only realistic options. The presence of the current dependency culture is a serious challenge to those trapped in it.

Unless the South Asian communities do something themselves, social disorders of the kind the city has been frequently experiencing since 1995 are likely to cause more damage to the communities themselves and to their relations with other communities. It is heartening to see the level of co-operation received by the police from the Muslim parents in identifying those involved in the street riots in 2001.

It can be argued that the South Asian communities and their leaders should seriously reflect on their own socio-economic position and community affairs. Such an exercise or investigation could be of the kind carried out by Bradford Metro Faith in the City Forum (12) or an exercise of the kind carried out by the Race Relations Advisory Group of Bradford Metropolitan Council in 1982, but it needs to be more comprehensive and ambitious. (13) The Ouseley Report has made a major recent contribution in highlighting some of the significant issues facing the city and in proposing an agenda for action.

The focus of thought and action in the city always appears to be on the "Muslim problem". There is little recognition of the fact that in reality the situation is much more complex. In the first place, it is neither Islam nor the entire Muslim community that is a 'problem'. Most of the law and order issues are concerned with the young people of a particular section of the Pakistani community that originates from the Azad Kashmir or Mirpur area of Pakistan. Furthermore, perceiving and presenting the issues in 'Muslim' terms has seriously alienated the Indian, African and Caribbean communities from race related issues. These communities feel marginalised in the city and seem to have effectively disengaged from the majority of local initiatives. Little attempt has been made to learn from the relatively successful educational and economic experiences of the local Hindu and Sikh communities.

Conclusion

Bradford faces a number of crucial issues in relation to the creation of harmonious race relations in the city and in providing equality of opportunity to minority ethnic communities. These issues include:

1. Bradford has a growing labour force, particularly from minority ethnic communities. How to create adequate and appropriate employment opportunities for a substantial number of young people particularly from ethnic minority communities is a fundamental issue for at least the next decade or so. The structure of the labour market of the District is substantially changed and this change continues to accelerate. The newly emerging strong sectors of service industries, financial and technological facilities, and tourism have to become 'all inclusive'. There is a good deal of rhetoric about the strengths and positive features of the District but, sadly there is little evidence so far of serious action to exploit these strengths in moving the agenda of economic regeneration forward.

The struggle for racial justice

Bradford's bid for *European Capital of Culture 2008* is a renewed this opening for the authorities to demonstrate that they can turn their dream into reality.

2. The educational underachievement of young people of Pakistani and Bangladeshi origin is a significant factor in the alienation of many of them, estrangement not only from the local situation but alienation from themselves too. The problems of these disaffected young people, particularly the boys, should be at the heart of policies designed to create high standard education and training facilities in the city. The piecemeal 'homework' projects set up by the community in some areas of the city to help youngsters in achieving qualification standards in schoolwork are encouraging.

3. Race and community relations, particularly in the inner city, are in a poor state. These relations are deteriorating further and further with the intermixing of other social problems such as prostitution, crime, drugs, gang-fights etc. The growing danger is the increasing belief of those living in the suburbs that these are the 'problems of minority communities', which they should deal with themselves, rather than the recognition that all such problems will prove intractable unless and until they are owned by the community at large.

4. The existence of serious racial inequalities in the city is adequately documented and is widely acknowledged. The high concentration of "under-class" minority communities in central Bradford is most likely to remain an issue for some decades to come. For a variety of social, cultural and economic reasons even the younger people from these communities are unlikely to move away from the cluster of their communities.

5. Past experience suggests that the sharp religious divisions between South Asians in Bradford hinder any effective co-operation and support in dealing with matters of common concern. Despite the fact that the Muslim communities in the city suffer considerably more from racial inequalities and from social disorder issues, other South

Asian communities, African and Caribbean communities and the Chinese community also have a stake in race relations. The urgency and importance of the cause deserves a serious attempt to bring all South Asians in the city to a common platform for the future of good race relations in the District.

There are no easy, readymade and quick-fix solutions to the problems that the city faces. There are some real impediments in the way of lessening the race inequalities and thus improving the race relations situation in the city. However, some immediate essential steps, if taken, can enormously assist in moving forward and tackling these broad issues.

First of all, an open, frank and fearless debate about the major issues needs to happen, beyond the boundaries of political expediency, electoral gain or community backlash. In this debate the minority communities' involvement must go beyond superficial consultation. It is argued that unless the local Muslim community and its leadership decides to root out the 'undesirable' elements of their own society with firmness, working in co-operation with the forces of law and other relevant agencies in the city, lasting peace in Bradford would remain a permanently distant dream. Otherwise, it is the local Muslim community of today and tomorrow that is likely to suffer the worst damage and remain an under-class for the foreseeable future.

Secondly, efforts have to be made initially and mainly by some minority communities themselves, to change the narrow and highly conservative religious and social visions to which they hold. Ethnic minority communities have to own some of the problems that are internal to them and accept the responsibility to play their part more vigorously in resolving them. Reports and some letters published in the T&A written by South Asian young people indicate an encouraging trend that awareness is increasing within the Muslim population about the issues that their community faces about which they need to own, debate within the community and initiate change.

Thirdly, parents and the community as a whole must become partners with the official agencies in the uplift of the poor level of educational attainment and participation in training by those who need it most and who are already at the bottom of the social scale.

Fourthly, politicians and local institutions have to demonstrate their courage in accepting the failure of certain past policies and projects and their willingness to undertake the critical assessment and monitoring of on-going projects. There is generally a lot more 'spin' about the new initiatives taken to deal with racial inequality than the reality at the ground level.

Finally, the serious question needs to be answered, and answered speedily is: how is the city going to implement the recommendations of the Ouseley Report and the Home Office Reports, and its policies of economic regeneration. Sadly, the progress on this front is unacceptably slow. It has to resolve the issue about how to co-ordinate the strategies and actions of a wide range of partners in the field, and to monitor the success or failure of their initiatives. It should also explore the question whether Bradford requires an independent organisation that should have an overarching responsibility for promoting good race relations in the District and for the monitoring of its policies and initiatives aimed at achieving racial equality. The following chapter attempts to address this question in some detail.

18

RACIAL JUSTICE CONGRESS:
A WAY FORWARD (1)

When the Bradford Racial Equality Council's doors were locked in March 2000 anger was expressed against Bradford Council and the CRE for withdrawing funding. Those who had a long-term association with it displayed sadness and shed some emotional tears. Speculations were made about the possible nasty political fall out from its demise. Two years on, the business of race relations in the city 'without' BREC appears to be as usual and *it does not seem to be missed*. Nevertheless, this is not an indication of a satisfactory state of race relations in the city. If that were the case, then there would have been no real reason for Bradford Council to launch a high level review into the future of racial equality in the District, at a cost of over £100,00 and with the collaboration of the Bradford Congress (now restructured as Bradford Vision). The Bradford District Race Review Panel (BDRRP) was expected to consider whether Bradford needed a racial equality organisation, and if it did, to identify the role, structure, and remit of such an organisation.

An analysis of the reasons behind the downfall of the BREC and the changed scenario for the existence of RECs nationally presented in the earlier chapters provide some serious points against the setting up of a replacement racial equality organisation on the traditional pattern. Among the cons, the arguments may include:

1. The white population and most mainstream organisations locally and nationally still perceive race relations agencies as organisations created for the protection of minority ethnic communities. This perception is confirmed as most RECs are currently controlled, managed and staffed by people of minority ethnic origin. Therefore, members of the white communities see their involvement as nominal, marginal and somewhat irrelevant.

2. There is also a view (however, a minority belief) that RECs have in fact delayed and hindered the development of direct links between the minority ethnic communities and local institutions. In their absence, the institutions would have been forced to forge links quickly and more realistically from necessity. Therefore, they should be removed from the scene.

3. Minority ethnic communities, despite some serious weaknesses in their own organisations, have become mature and confident enough to represent their own perspectives on most race related issues. Thus, they do not feel the same need for an intermediary such as a REC as they did, say fifteen years ago. Furthermore, over the years, the development of ethnic minority umbrella organisations among Hindu, Sikh and Muslim communities at the local level have strengthened their positions in this respect even further.

4. The last decade has witnessed an increased number of people from minority ethnic communities becoming involved with the political processes and seeking offices in political institutions. These people are now able to raise the appropriate concerns of minority communities at all stages of the political decision making processes. The elected members may rightly claim that they are the legitimate and true representatives of their communities. They have increasingly started challenging the authority of traditional (unelected) community leaders on whose contribution and commitment local race bodies have relied for so long.

5. Overall, the interest of minority ethnic communities in the work of the race relations organisations has weakened, as the Bradford experience typically highlights. Such bodies have been unable to attract and involve women and the younger generation of minority ethnic communities. The popular media project a very negative and undesirable image of race relations agencies by referring to them as the 'race industry'. Therefore, high calibre young black and Asians show no aspiration to seek career in the field of race relations. Furthermore, the younger generation growing up in Britain has gained knowledge of mainstream systems and developed familiarity

with the working of local institutions. They feel their own and their parents need for assistance from organisations such as RECs has diminished.

6. Despite the existence of race prejudice, racial discrimination and racial disadvantages the experience of racism of different communities varies. The nature, level and impact of inequalities are significantly different for individual minority communities. This diversity in experience has direct implications for the interest, commitment and involvement of different communities in the field of race relations generally and in the activities of bodies specifically concerned with race relations.

7. At best gradually, the traditional roles of local race equality organisations have changed significantly. For instant, the issues around immigration and nationality have become less urgent for the established minority ethnic communities. Therefore, the casework role that justified the existence of many RECs in relation to welfare, immigration and nationality has not only lost its significance but has been taken over either by other voluntary community based organisations or by public sector advisory bodies. With the appointment of equal opportunity officers by most major public and private sector organisations, the educational and promotional roles of the RECs have already become less significant.

8. The 1990s have experienced a significant change in organisations' approach to equal opportunity policies. Most organisations, like Bradford Council, have stopped developing separate equality policies for race and gender. They have merged such policies under the generic title "equal rights" policy, which embraces even their policies on ageism, disability and sexual orientation. The new approach to race equality issues is advocated on "commercial, economic and legal" determinants, with the moral responsibility argument taking a marginal position. Within this approach, it becomes difficult to justify a separate body to deal with *only* race and cultural diversity related concerns.

In the specific context of Bradford, some of the traditional functions of the BREC are currently being performed by statutory and voluntary organisations. For example, at present organisations exist that provide training in racism awareness, cultural awareness and equal opportunities. Multi-agency units exist to monitor racial harassment; the Law Centre and the Northern Aids Fund take up racial discrimination cases, and a good deal of general advice and welfare related casework is carried out by advice workers in local authority funded community centres and the CAB. Information and data on current racial issues are easily available from the research efforts of many national and local organisations. Ethnic minority organisations have matured and most of them are well informed and confident enough to present needs to the appropriate agencies. Now they even demonstrate their courage and capacity to fight for the legitimate rights of their members.

Racial Justice Congress
In Bradford, minority ethnic communities have developed their distinctive separate identities, and live and function socially and religiously in isolation. Interaction between ethnically diverse local communities is poor and superficial, if at all. The cases of race disturbances and racial attacks are significant and happen too often. Race inequalities are obvious and firmly entrenched. Despite the strong arguments presented above that go against the establishment of another BREC for the District there is a potential role for an agency of some sort in fostering cross community interaction in order to reverse the polarisation of communities that has taken place. Nevertheless, a small body on its own, can only makes a marginal contribution. This is an area for action through partnership between all private and public sector institutions and agencies.

In considering the case for establishing such an organisation it would be imperative to take account of the current state of race equality and cultural diversity in the city, and of the lessons that could be learnt from the weaknesses of the policies of race relations of the past fifty years in the city. To depart from the past, I would suggest a new model and a new name for such an organisation. It could be called the Racial Justice Congress (RJC) and should have a broad brief to deal with race equality issues in the District. In determining the precise nature of its responsibilities, sphere of operation and activities, answers to the following specific questions may assist:

♦ *How effectively the organisations that currently deal with race and diversity related matters perform their roles? Where are the gaps in their services?*
♦ *What a small race equality organisation (if set up) with limited human, professional and financial resources can effectively do?*
♦ *What would be the expectations of the potential main funding organisations i.e. the CRE, local authority together with those of local communities including ethnic minority communities?*

The answers to these questions at present do not exist. It was hoped that the work of the Bradford District Race Review Panel (BDRRP) will provide some direction in this area. However, the Ouseley Report conspicuously fails to provide any specific, precise and practical answer beyond some broad generalisations.

I would suggest that the role of the RJC should be guided by three broad objectives:
• *to work towards the elimination of racial discrimination;*
• *to promote equality of opportunity, and good relations between persons of different racial groups; and*
• *to empower ethnic minority communities both for self-help and to speak for themselves.*

RJC should adopt a more strategic, co-ordinating, supporting and independent monitoring role in the development of policies to eliminate racial inequalities, for lessening racial tensions and for promoting harmonious inter community relations. It should attempt to achieve its objectives working through effective partnership and by demolishing the 'conspiracy of silence' on race related matters from which the city has suffered in the past. It should take a broader and comprehensive view of race equality issues and work neutrally and independently of local political pressures.

These objectives may be achieved through specific functions which may include all or some of these:

1. *To work towards the elimination of racial discrimination, racial prejudice, racial harassment and racial inequalities, on the principle of shared responsibility with its partners.*
2. *To take a strategic overview of the current and future policies of its partner agencies.*
3. *To take a resource efficient coordinating role in the development of race related policies of its member organisations.*
4. *To encourage, advise and support its partners in working towards the achievement of the above three broad objectives.*
5. *To act as a watchdog in the field of race equality and cultural diversity matters, to challenge and question organisational responses in these areas.*
6. *To provide minority ethnic communities with a forum where they can share experiences and common concerns with policy makers and service providers.*
7. *To raise the awareness of individuals and organisations about racial inequalities and racial discrimination.*
8. *To work towards weakening self-segregation and cultural divisiveness, and increasing community cohesion.*

In structural terms the RJC's partners should include major public sector and voluntary organisations, umbrella minority ethnic organisations and a fairly small number of high-profile individual members with commitment to and expertise in race relations. The management board of the RJC must reflect a secular, non-partisan, all inclusive and neutral composition. It should be a small size organisation headed by a director of highest integrity and proven management and public relations skills. He/she should have a track record of the working with major organisations and ethnic minority communities.

NOTES

Chapter 1

1. Two excellent examples of work of the Bradford Heritage Recording Unit are its publications: *Destination Bradford: A Century of Immigration*, 1987; *and Here To Stay: Bradford's South Asian Communities*, 1994.
2. McNeil Frances (Ed) (1997), *Such a Journey: Bradford Peace Stories Project: Stories, Poems and Memories From Bradford People*, Bradford Libraries, Bradford.

Chapter 2

1. *Home Affairs Committee of the House of Commons, Session 1980/81, Racial Disadvantage Vol. I, July 1981, PP.XXXVI-XXXVII*
2. *The Lord Scarman Report: The Brixton Disorder, 10-12 April, 1981;* HMSO, Nov. 1981, pp.110-111
3. See for example, *The Independent*, 14 June 1990.
4. *The Sunday Times*, 17 June 1990.
5. See for example, Nigerian born publisher, Glory Osaji-Umeaku, *Ethnic Enterprise News* and *The Daily Mail*, 13 June 1990.
6. David Blunkett, the Home Secretary in *Connections*, Summer 2001, Quarterly Journal of the Commission for Racial Equality, page 3.
7. *Connections*, Summer 2001, Quarterly Journal of the Commission for Racial Equality, page 4.

Chapter 3

1. In the early part of 1976, the Telegraph & Argus printed a series of short articles by: John Salmon on Muslims, Esther Leach on Ukrainians, Rodney Hopkinson on Byelorussian, Malcolm Flanagan on Hungarian, Latvians and Chinese, Martin Wainright on Jews and Poles, Viktar Buseucs on Jews and Chris Walker on Irish. Number of sources e.g. Richardson (1976), Jowitt and Perks (1987), Singh (1986, 1992, 1994, 1997, 2000) included in the bibliography provide fairly comprehensive information, adequate for ordinary

readers on most of the minority ethnic communities in the city with the exception of African-Caribbean community.

2. For a detailed account of the South Asian communities' presence and settlement in Bradford see *Introduction* by Ramindar Singh in *Here To Stay: Braford's South Asian Communities*, Bradford Heritage Unit, City of Bradford Metro. Council, Arts, Museums and Libraries, 1994.

Chapter 9

1. See the report of a formal investigation by the Commission for Racial Equality (June 1983): *The Bradford District of the West Yorkshire Passenger Transport (Bradford Metro) Report of a Formal Investigation.*

Chapter 10

1. For a brief overview see Ishtiaq Ahmed, *The Quest For Racial Justice In Bradford*, in Carol Rank (Ed) *City Of Peace: Bradford's Story*, Bradford Libraries, 1997.

2. See Molly Kenyon, *Healing the Wounds: Bradford After the Disturbances of 9-11 June 1995*, Faith To Faith Project, Touchstone, 1995.

3. Most of the information about the West Indian organisations is gleaned from a file of press cuttings on West Indian community kept by the Central Library, Bradford.

4. Bradford Congress was renamed and restructured as Bradford Vision towards at the end of 2000.

Chapter 11

1. For instance, Sukhdev Sharma who worked as an Assistant CRO, became the Executive Director of the CRE, Ramindar Singh became a Joint Deputy Chairman of the CRE, Tim Whitfield, Frank Henley and Bhula Singh and many more hold senior positions with Bradford Council. Marsha Singh, one time a junior officer in BREC, has become the first Bradford Asian MP and Mohammed Ajeeb, the first Asian chairman of Bradford CRC became the first Asian Lord Mayor in the UK. Mohammed Ali, a junior officer of the CRC, is

now the Chief Executive of a nationally known independent organisation, QED.

2. The panel was set up under the chairmanship of Tom Crehan, Headmaster of Belle Vue Grammar School. During its 18 years of continuous working Mr R Parwaz (1971-73), Ramindar Singh (1973-83), Ranjit Kaur Arora (1983-84) and Mrs J Baruch (1984-86) chaired the Panel. For most of the time the Panel was serviced by the Education CRO, Swaran Singh Badan.

3. Mr M A Seed Khan was its first Chairman. Marsha Singh revived the Panel in 1979 and it continued its struggle for existence under the chairmanship of John Prestige (1982-83) and Terry Rickhuss (1983-87).

4. Dr Phillip Rack (1974-81), Dr H K Shah (1974-79) and Miss I Senior (1979-1982) chaired the Panel jointly during their respective periods of office. Mr N S Farrar (1982-85) and Mr D Khan (1985-86) were the two last chairs of the panel.

5. Chief Superintendent Roper (1981-82), Chief Superintendent Morrit (1982-83) and Chief Superintendent Alderson (1983-85) chaired the Panel during the 1980s.

Chapter 12

1. See Bradford Metro Council (1981), *The Turning Points: A Review of Race Relations in Bradford*, Page 7

2. *The 12 Point Plan* Of 1981 was changed to *The 18 Point Plan* in 1986 by the Labour Group. See Appendix B for plan and policy documents.

3. See Thomas Sowell, *Race and Econmics*, David Mckay Co., New York and John Mjewski, *The Economics of Race and Discrimination*, Economic Affairs, February/March, 1988.

Chapter 13

1. See T.F.Davies, *Educational Problems in Bradford*, in Immigration-Medical and Social Aspects, A Ciba Foundation Report, 1966.

2. *Turning Point: A Review of Race Relations in Bradford*, Bradford Metro Council, 1981.

3. The Ofsted Report: *Inspection Of Bradford Local Education Authority, May 2000*, pages 40-42.

The struggle for racial justice

Chapter 14

1. Peter Ratcliffe et.al., *Breaking Down the Barriers: Improving Asian Access to Social Rented Housing*, published by the Charted Institute of Housing, 2001.

Chapter 15

1. Councillor Marget Eaton, Conservative Leader of Bradford Council quoted in the T&A, 30 July 2001.
2. The report covers a wide range of concerns about police, the local economy, the public and media image if the city, long-standing issues in education and so on. The small selection of concerns mentioned here relates to those that significantly impact on the state of race relations in the city.
3. The report provides a good deal of detail about the aims, objectives, contents and the possible organisational structure for these features of the proposed programme.
4. Bradford has the experience of having a Bussing Policy and Language Centres for the education of non-English speaking children in the 1960s and the1970s. It had a high profile multicultural education and equal opportunity policies; racism awareness training programmes; an active Racial Equality Council for 35 years; community grants programmes for the minority ethnic communities' initiatives and so on. None of these policies and programmes had an unqualified success (see chapters 12 and 13)

Chapter 16

1. The contents of the two reports overlap and are complementary in most ways. They need to be read together to fully appreciate the proposed direction for action to redress the serious issues raised by the race riots last summer (2001) and the state of racial and religious segregation in cities such as Bradford.

2. An analysis of the concept of community cohesion written by Dr Rosalyn Lynch is contained in Appendix C of the Cantle Report.

186

Chapter 17

1. Some of the material contained in this chapter was presented to the Bradford Commission in 1995 and to the Bradford Race Review Panel chaired by Sir Herman Ouseley in 2001.
2. *District and Ward 1991 Census Digest*, Bradford Metropolitan Council Report.
3. *Powerful Whisper*, Bradford Metro Faith in the City Forum, 1995.
4. See *Areas of Stress within Bradford District*, Bradford Metropolitan Council Report, October 1993, pp. 8-19.
5. *District and Ward 1991 Census Digest*, Bradford Metropolitan Council.
6. *Bradford in Brief* (1993), Bradford Metropolitan Council.
7. *Areas of Stress within Bradford District* a report by Research Section of the Chief Executive's Department, Bradford Metro Council, dated October 1993 based on the 1991 Census data using 18 indicators of poverty or multiple stress.
8. *A Fair Deal For Bradford*, Bradford Metropolitan Council, 1995
9. *Bradford & District Economic Profile 1995*, Bradford & District Training and Enterprise Council, 1995, p. 17.
10. *Telegraph & Argus*, 21 November 1995.
11. *A Fair Deal For Bradford*, Bradford Metropolitan Council, 1995
12. *Powerful Whispers*, Bradford Metro Faith in the City Forum, 1995.
13. *The Other Man's View*, Bradford Metropolitan Council, April 1982.

Chapter 18

1. A shortened version of this chapter was submitted to the Bradford Race Review Panel chaired by Sir Herman Ouseley in 2001. The proposal for setting up a Centre for Diversity, Learning and Living in the city recommended by the Ouseley Report has captured most of the central ideas forwarded in the proposal here.

The struggle for racial justice

Bibliography and References

The story of Bradford 1950-2002

Bradford Metropolitan Council (1981) *Turning Points: A review of Race relations in Bradford*

Bradford Metropolitan Council (1982) *A Chance To Speak*, Report of the RRAG & SEAG

Bradford Metropolitan Council (1982) *The Other Man's View*

Bradford Metropolitan Council (1987) *Towards Education for All*, Directorate of Education Services

Bradford Metropolitan Council (1993) *Areas of Stress within Bradford District*, pp. 1 8-19

Bradford Metropolitan Council (1993) *Bradford Economic Review*, No 1, Spring 1993, Census Special

Bradford Metropolitan Council (1993) *Bradford in Brief*

Bradford Metropolitan Council (1995) *A Fair Deal For Bradford*

Bradford Metropolitan Council (1996) *Population Estimates in Bradford District*, Corporate Services, Research Section

Bradford Metropolitan Council (1997) *Response to the Bradford Commission Reports*, 25th March

Bradford Metropolitan Council (1997) *Population Estimates in Bradford District, July 1997*

Bradford Metropolitan Council (2000) *Cultural Diversity in Practice: A good Practice Guide For Schools*, Bradford Education Services

Bradford Metropolitan Council (undated) *District and Ward 1991 Census Digest*

Bradford Metropolitan Council (undated) *Race Relations In Bradford: The Council's Approach*, Policy Unit

The struggle for racial justice

Bradford Metropolitan Council (undated) *Making a Difference: Best Value Performance Plan 200-2001*, Strategic Support Division

Brown, Andrew (1985) *Trials of Honerford: Problems in Multicultural Education*, Centre For Policy Studies, Pilot Paper No. 2

Cantle, Ted (2001) *Community Cohesion: A Report of the Independent Review Team*, Home Office, London

Carr, John (1993) *"Alibis For Inaction": A report for the Chief Executive*, Bradford Metropolitan Council, Bradford

Christmas, Linda (1989) *Chopping Down The Cherry Tree: A Portrait of Britain in the Eighties*, Chapter 9, Bradford: The Police-'If you print that I'll deny that I said it', Viking, London

Commission for Racial Equality (1983) *The Bradford District of the West Yorkshire Passenger Transport (Bradford Metro) Report of a Formal Investigation*, London

Foundation 2000 (1995) *The Disturbances in Mannigham: A Community Response: The Voices Must Be Heard*, Foundation 2000, Bradford.

Gay, Pat and Young, Ken (1988) *Community Relations Councils: Roles and Objectives*, Policy Studies Institute and Commission for Racial Equality, London

Halstead, M (1988) *Education, Justice and Cultural Diversity: An Examination of the Honeyford Affair, 1984-85*, Falmer, London

Hill, M J and Issacharoff, R M (1971) *Community Action and Race Relations*, OUP for IRR, London

Home Affairs Committee of the House of Commons, *Session 1980/81, Racial Disadvantage Vol.I, July 1981, PP.XXXVI-XXXVII*

Home Office (1981) *Report On Racial Attacks*, Home Office, London

Home Office (2001) *Building Cohesive Communities: A Report of the Ministerial Group on Public Order and Community Cohesion*, London

Home Office (2001) *Community Cohesion: A Report of the Independent Review Team*, London

Jowitt, J A and Perks, R B (1987) Introduction, in *Destination Bradford*, Bradford Heritage Recording Unit, Bradford Metro Council, Bradford.

Kenyon, Molly (1995) *Healing the Wounds: Bradford After the Disturbances of 9-11 June 1995*, Faith to Faith Project, Touchstone, Bradford

Lewis, Philip (1992) *Beyond Babel: An Anglican Perspective in Bradford: The Eighth Lambeth Interfaith Lecture*, Lambeth Palace, London, 17th November

Lewis, Philip (1994) *Islamic Britain: Religion, Politics and Identity among British Muslims: Bradford in the 1990s*, I.B. Tauris, London

Markowitz, L M (1994) The Cross-Currents of Multiculturalism, in *The Family Network*, July/August

McNaiel, Frances (Ed) (1997) *Such a Journey: Bradford Peace Stories Project: Stories, Poems and Memories From Bradford People*, Bradford Libraries, Bradford

Mehdood, Tariq (1983) *Hand On The Sun*, Penguin, Harmondsworth, England

Mjewski, John (1988) The Econmics of Race and Discrimination, *Economic Affairs*, February/March

Murphy, Dervala (1987) *Tales From Two Cities: Travel of Another Sort*, John Murray, London

Ouseley, Herman (2001) *Community Pride Not Prejudice: Making Diversity Work in Bradford*, Bradford Vision, Bradford

Parekh, Bhikhu (2000) *The Future of Multi-Ethnic Britain: The Parekh Report*, The Runnymede Trust, London

Rank, Carol (Ed) (1997) *City Of Peace: Bradford's Story*, Bradford Libraries, Bradford

Ratcliffe, Peter (1996) *Race and Housing in Bradford, Addressing the needs of the South Asian, African and Caribbean communities*, Bradford Housing Forum, Bradford

Ratcliffe, Peter et. al. (2001) *Breaking Down the Barriers: Improving Asian Access to Social Rented Housing*, Charted Institute of Housing, Coventry

Richardson, Clem (1976) *A Geography of Bradford*, University of Bradford, Bradford

Samad, Yunas (1992) Book Burning and Race Relations: Political Mobilisation of Bradford Muslims, *New Community*, 18 (4), July

Scarman, L (1981) *The Scarman Report:The Brixton Disorder, 10-12 April, 1981*, HMSO,London

Sewell, Thomas (undated) *Race and Economics*, David Mckay Co., New York

Singh, Ramindar with Ram, Sodhi, (1986) *Indians in Bradfod:. The Development of a Community*, Bradford & llkley Community College, Bradford

Singh, Ramindar (1992) *Immigrants To Citizens: The Sikh Community In Bradford*, Bradford & llkley Community College, Bradford

Singh, Ramindar (1994)   Introduction in *Here To Stay: Bradford's South Asian Communities*, Bradford Heritage Recording Unit, Bradford

Singh, Ramindar (1997) Understanding Bradford's South Asian Community in Carol Rank (Ed.) *City of Peace: Bradford's Story*, Bradford Libraries, Bradford.

Singh, Ramindar (2000) *Sikhs & Sikhism in Britain: Fifty Years On: the Bradford Perspective*, Bradford Libraries, Bradford

Taj, M (1996) *A'Can Do' City, Supplementary Observations, Comments and recommendations To The Bradford Commission Report*, Bradford Congress, Bradford

Newspapers and Journals
Connections, Spring 2001, Quarterly Journal of the Commission for Racial equality, London
New Community, July 1992
The Daily Mail, 13 June 1990
The Economic Affairs, February/March 1988
The Family Network, July August 1988
The Guardian, 11 July 1989
The Independent, 14 June 1990
The New Statesman and Society, 10 January 1992
The Telegraph & Argus, various dates as indicated in the main text.

Appendix A

HONORARY OFFICERS OF THE BRADFORD RACIAL EQUALITY COUNCIL
(Previously Bradford Community Relations Council)

Year	Chairman	Vice Chairmen	Treasurer
1999-00	Mrs Lynne Kent	Mr Fazal Haq Mr H K Shah	Mr D D Sharma
1998-99	Mr Balbir Singh JP	Mr Fazal Haq Mr H K Shah	Mr D D Sharma
1995-98	Mr Balbir Singh JP	Mr Fazal Haq Mr H K Shah	Mr D D Sharma
1994-95	Mr Balbir Singh JP	Mr Fazal Haq Mr H K Shah	Mr G Singh
1993-94	Mr Balbir Singh JP	Mr Fazal Haq Mr M A Salam	Mr D D Sharma
1992-93	Ms R Burhan	Cllr Balbir Singh Mr Fazal Haq	Mr D D Sharma
1991-92	Mr Govinder Singh Dhaliwal	Cllr Balbir Singh Mr Fazal Haq	Mr P Chong
1990-91	Mr Govinder Singh Dhaliwal	Mr J Martin Mr M Ali	Mr P Chong
1989-90	Mr M A Salam	Mr I Ahmed Cllr Balbir Singh	Mrs P Parbhakar
1988-89	Mr I Ahmed	Mr R Parmar Mr M A Salam	Mr K K Mittal
1987-88	Mr I Ahmed	Mr R Parmar Mr M A Salam	Mr K K Mittal
1986-87	Cllr A R Hameed	Mr R Parmar Mr C M Khan	Mr K K Mittal
1985-86	Cllr A R Hameed	Mr R Parmar Mr Dhian Singh Bharaj	Cllr M Riaz
1984-85	Cllr A R Hameed	Mr R P Johar Mr John Samuel	Mr M Riaz

1983-84	Mr Ramindar Singh JP	Cllr Abdul Hameed Mr John Samuel	MR K K Mittal
1982-83	Cllr Mohammed Ajeeb	Mr R P Johar	Mr K K Mittal
1981-82	Cllr Mohammed Ajeeb	Mr R P Johar	Cllr Abdul Hameed
1980-81	Cllr Mohammad Ajeeb	Mr R P Johar	Mr Mewa Singh Bussan JP
1979-80	Cllr Mohammad Ajeeb	Dr Philip Rack	Rt Rev Mgr M V Sweeney
1978-79	Mr Mohammed Ajeeb	Rabbi M Heilbron	Rt Rev Mgr M V Sweeney
1977-78	Mr Mohammed Ajeeb	Dr Philip Rack	Rt Rev Mgr M V Sweeney
1976-77	Mr Mohammed Ajeeb	Dr Philip Rack	Rt Rev Mgr M V Sweeney
1975-76	Mr Tom Crehan JP	Miss E Rawson Dr H K Shah	Rt Rev Mgr M V Sweeney
1974-75	Mr Tom Crehan JP	Dr H K Shah	Rt Rev Mgr M V Sweeney
1973-74	Mr Tom Crehan JP	Dr H K Shah	Rt Rev Mgr M V Sweeney
1972-73	Mr Tom Crehan JP	Dr H K Shah	Mr R N W Bishop
1971-72	Mr Tom CrehanJP	Mr Rana M R K Parwaz	Mr R N W Bishop
1970-71	The Rt Rev Michael Parker	Dr S Hussain Qureshi	Mr R N W Bishop
1969-70	The Rt Rev Michael Parker	Dr M Tahir Qureshi	Mr R N W Bishop
1968-69	The Rt Rev Michael Parker	Mr M Saeed Khan	Mr R N W Bishop
1967-68	The Rt Rev Michael Parker	Mr M Saeed Khan	Mr R N W Bishop
1966-67	The Rt Rev Michael Parker	Mr M Saeed Khan	Mr Henery Patton Town Clerk

Appendix B
Policy statements: 1

Race Relations
The 12 Point Plan

Bradford Council pledges itself to take all necessary steps as a major employer, provider of services and influence on public opinion to improve race relations in our city.

We commit ourselves to encouraging equal opportunities and fighting 'both racial discrimination and racial disadvantage with positive action now.

We also recognise we are a multi-racial, multi-cultural city and that every section of the community has an equal right to maintain its own identity, culture, language, religion and customs.

We believe these ties of culture and ethnic loyalty are an asset to Bradford and we promise to take them into account in planning our services.

The Council will:

1. Adopt an equal opportunity employment policy;
2. Make all employees aware of the part they play in promoting racial equality;
3. Keep ethnic records to check up on our activities;
4. Take into account the special needs of ethnic minorities when providing services;
5. Make sure all racial and ethnic groups have an equal chance to use our services and facilities;
6. Fight racial discrimination and encourage other employers to do the same;
7. Improve communications with ethnic communities and involve them when we make decisions which affect them;
8. Support our local Community Relations Council;
9. Encourage ethnic minority self-help initiatives;
10. Seek government and Common Market money for special schemes for the ethnic minorities;
11. Speak out on national race relations issues;
12. Ask our Committees and Sub-Committees to consult with our Race Relations Advisory Group before making decisions on any policies affecting race relations.

Appendix B

Policy statements: 2

City of Bradford Metropolitan Council
Race Relations And The Council

Dear Employee,

You may have read in the Press that Bradford Met has adopted a new policy on race relations and you may have wondered what it involves and how it affects you at work. As the leaders of the Council's three political groups we are writing to all our employees to tell you more about it.

Very briefly, the policy aims to improve race relations through the ways in which we employ people, provide services and influence the local community. We say that fair treatment and respect for each other's differences are keys to greater understanding and racial harmony. We no longer expect minority communities to integrate and change their ways to suit us. Bradford has many communities and each has an equal right to maintain its own distinct life-style, religion, language and customs.

In addition, as ratepayers the members of each community have an equal right to Council services and facilities according to their needs.

We recognise these rights and expect our committees and staff to do the same. Good race relations, in a city such as Bradford, are far too important to leave to chance any longer.

That is why we have committed ourselves to a policy to encourage equal opportunities, to reduce racial disadvantage, and to root out once and for all racial discrimination. That is also why we have set up a Race Relations Advisory Group of Councillors to make sure our intentions are actually put into effect.

More details about our policy are summarised in the 12-point plan over the page.

One of the key sections of the plan is an equal opportunity employment policy. At the moment only 2% of our employees are from ethnic minority groups although they make up about 15% of the district's population. We need to aim for a fairer balance between our workforce and the communities we serve.

The struggle for racial justice

This means that everyone, regardless of race, creed or colour, should have an equal chance to get a council job based solely on individual merit and suitability. We now need to take a hard look at how we advertise jobs to attract applicants and at how interviewing panels work to make sure that we are not favouring certain groups in appointments.

We have started to examine the reasons people are rejected and the qualifications and qualities we demand for our jobs. To make sure that we actually put our policies into practice we are keeping record of all our selection decisions to check on our progress.

If you would like further details, please ring Bradford 729577 extension 7720 and ask for a copy of the "Race Relations Policy Statement" or the report "Race and Employment in Bradford Metropolitan Council".
We believe every employee is affected by these new policies. They have the backing of the law and we intend to uphold them vigorously. Whether you meet the public, make decisions, supervise or recruit staff or provide a service we believe it is important for you to understand what we aim to do.

Whilst realistically we do not expect to achieve all our objectives overnight we are pledged to achieve a fair and just society with equal opportunities for all. We need your help and co-operation to make sure we succeed.
Yours sincerely

Leader Conservative Group   Leader Labour Group   Leader Liberal Group

Policy statements: 3

City of Bradford Metropolitan Council
Race Relations Policy in Bradford

Race Relations

Race Relations is not a static issue, circumstances change, views and attitudes change. Policies must be dynamic if they are to meet new situations.

Our primary objective is simple but ambitious:-

To create a society in which there is co-operative and peaceful living together based on mutual respect for differences, a society that is genuinely multi-racial. This can be achieved only by an equality of treatment, an equality of opportunity, equality of services and without discrimination based on race, religion or culture. We seek a society in which there is unity but not uniformity.

In order to achieve this objective we must set ourselves a series of more specific goals. They are:-

1. To ensure that the Council is able to respond quickly and effectively to racism when it appears.
2. To seek a society in which nobody in the Bradford District is subject to racial harassment or discrimination.
3. To create an environment in which the various cultures and beliefs which exist in the Bradford District can do so in peace and with mutual respect.
4. To ensure that all Council employees are fully aware of the Council's race relations policies, why they exist and what their responsibilities are towards the promotion of racial equality.
5. To ensure that the citizens of the Bradford District are aware of the Council's policies and why they exist.
6. To increase the number of people from the ethnic minority communities employed by the Council at all levels.
7. To ensure that other employers and agencies are aware of their responsibilities and to encourage them to engage in programmes to combat prejudice and discrimination.
8. To ensure that information about the Council's services is provided in a clear way and in a language appropriate to the communities being served.
9. To ensure that the services the Council is required to provide are appropriate to meet the needs of Bradford Districts diverse community and that access to these services is open to all.
10. To ensure that there are effective structures with the necessary support to institute and maintain powerful monitoring systems. The Council will maintain ethnic records as a means of monitoring the council's activities, and as a means of identifying possible areas of inequality.

11. To ensure that all the ethnic minority communities have equal opportunity to achieve their full potential particularly in the field of education.
12. To encourage community development and self help initiatives within the minority communities particularly in the development of employment and economic initiatives.
13. To ensure that the double disadvantage endured by ethnic minority women is recognised and addressed by all the Council's functions and their views are taken into account.
14. To ensure that when decisions are taken affecting the lives of the minority communities particularly in the allocation of resources that their views and needs are considered in the decision making process.
15. To ensure that central government is aware of the needs of the minority communities particularly on issues of national importance to good race relations.
16. To ensure that the special resources available from central government and the EEC are used to meet the needs of the minority communities in the most effective way.
17. To encourage the work of the Community Relations Council.
18. To ensure that all Committees and Sub-Committees consult with the Race Relations Advisory Group and all the relevant Race Relations Working Parties on all policy matters relating to race relations before final decisions are taken.

We will not achieve these objectives overnight. They are goals to aim for, but, without these goals we will not be able to measure our own performance.

Policy statements: 4

Conservative Election Statement
Confidential Second Draft
Race Relations

Our policy is based on the firm acceptance of the fact that Bradford Met District is now a city of diverse cultures. We recognise that all sections of the community have a right to a distinctive cultural identity based on the traditions of race, ethnic origin, language, custom and religion. Such identity exists independently of any formal acceptance by Local or Central Government.

The Conservative policy recognises a commitment to a society in which service provision is made irrespective of race, colour or creed, and to this end we would:-

a) Accept that a successful society requires mutual respect for and communication between constituent cultures.

b) Maintain that an individual has both the right and a duty to contribute to the building of one nation in Britain.

c) Support the maintenance of an equal opportunity employment policy by the Council, and be committed to a monitored programme of action to see that the policy is fully effective. As a step towards this we would end the Council's internal preference employment policy,

d) Ensure that all Directorates provide services relevant to such a society and ensure that within these services no individuals should find themselves at .o disadvantage because of their culture. In making service provision, build on the strengths of the various cultural groups.

e) State that our service provision is to meet individual needs. We recognise that individuals are entitled to choose their own life style. It is not our intention or role to artificially preserve cultures.

f) Continue an aggressive policy to Central Government and EEC funding in relationship to ethnic minority provision, and discuss with Central Government equal opportunities issues relevant to all the people of Bradford.

g) Ensure that all young people are equipped with the necessary skills with which to face the opportunities and challenges of British society. In order that the opportunities of British society are equal, all our young people must have the fundamental communication skill of fluency in the English language.

h) Recognise, and avoid, the dangers of creating potential divisions arising from separate systems of funding service for different client groups. We specifically reject a dual system of service provision.

i) Encourage positive attitudes towards self-reliance and wealth-creation, recognising that greater prosperity is a key to self-esteem and confidence for all groups within our society.

j) Within the terms of this document be prepared to debate alternative methods of policy implementation, and to acknowledge dissenting views. An effective race relation policy can only operate on the basis of consent.

k) Centre our activity on areas and issues for which the Council has responsibility. To this end we will concentrate our efforts on service provision through the Directorates of the Council.

Policy statements: 5

Equal Rights Statement

Bradford Metropolitan Council abhors all forms of discrimination, injustice and inequality. As a community led Council, we aim to ensure that all members of the community are able to exercise their rights to services and employment. We are committed to the elimination of all forms of discrimination and to creating equality of opportunity for everyone whatever their gender, race, disability, culture, religious beliefs, age, sexuality, class, economic or other disadvantage.

The Council recognises that all members of the community have the right to a high standard of housing, education, training, social services, transport, health and other services and that these should be provided equitably throughout the district on the basis of need. The Council is committed to ensuring that no individual within the community is excluded from these services.
As a major employer in the district Bradford Metropolitan Council has a responsibility to ensure that it provides equality of opportunity at all levels of employment, promotion and training for all members of the community.
We believe that all people have the right to access employment. We will create an atmosphere of mutual respect between employees and the community we serve and we will continually monitor and review our procedures to ensure that there are no discriminatory practises.

This policy will be actively pursued at all levels of the Council to ensure that the needs of all the people in the district are met. By working and consulting with the community and the Trade Unions we will continually revise and upgrade our policies and procedures to ensure that they are equitable and fair. It is the responsibility of the Council, each of its Committees and Directorates to ensure that this policy is implemented.

October 1991

INDEX